A Sky full of Stars

Know Our Lady through her titles in the Litany

JOBY PROVIDO

ISBN: 978-1793469236

2nd Printing
Printed and Published by
Kindlings Press

Nihil Obstat

Fr. Ronald M. Roberto
Minister for Liturgical Affairs

Imprimatur

+Honesto F. Ongtioco, D.D
Bishop of Cubao.

22 November 2018

The Nihil Obstat and Imprimatur are official declarations that a book or pamphlet is free of doctrinal or moral error.

No implication is contained therein that those who have granted the Nihil Obstat and Imprimatur agree with the contents, opinions, or statements expressed.

What People are Saying

" A Sky Full of Stars must be an obligatory reference material for religion teachers and seminarians. It helps the reader to see the Virgin Mary within the perspective of sound biblical theology and solid Catholic tradition... [and is] also easy to understand.

It happens quite often that Catholic devotion to the Virgin Mary suffers due to ignorance and grave lack of understanding [, and] many fall prey to fundamentalist sects and anti-Catholic tides. This book answers that need. It makes no attempt to be defensive but has chosen what we call 'positive orthodoxy', presenting the faith in its original clarity.

+Bishop Socrates Villegas
Archbishop Lingayen, Dagupan

Table of Contents

PREFACE

W HEN I WAS A CHILD, our family said the rosary together, and just like most kids, I felt the time spent on praying it was already too long. So when my mother introduced the litany that is usually said after the mysteries, the more I didn't look forward to "rosary time" because it took longer to get done.

Of course, that is no longer my sentiment today. I want to think that the way I pray the rosary has changed for the better over the years. But some of Our Lady's titles in the Litany continued to trouble me because I didn't know what they meant. These are titles like *Mystical Rose, Tower of David, Tower of Ivory, House of Gold, Gate of Heaven, and Morning Star* to name a few. No one could explain to me what they meant, so it felt a little bit empty and odd invoking them without understanding them.

To remedy this, I looked up the different meanings of the titles over the years. They were mostly pious expressions, and while there is nothing wrong with that, they did not explain the titles. The internet came to the rescue when it pointed me to a book, written in 1957 by Fr. Lawrence G. Lovasik, entitled *Our Lady in Catholic Life*. It is a prayer book where I found out that the different titles of our Lady were honored on each Saturday. More importantly, Fr. Lovasik's introduction to the titles captured the background and meaning of most of them. The book is no longer in print and can be very difficult to find, so I was thrilled to purchase a second-hand copy through book dealers.

This pursuit led me to Church documents, encyclicals, as well as commentaries on some of Our Lady's titles by St. Alphonsus Liguori, Blessed John Henry Newman, and St. Bernard of Clairvaux.

One of the revelations of this search is that some titles of Our Lady explode with meaning when attached to their contexts in Old Testament episodes, culture, and temple worship. Early Christians

1

and the Church Fathers made these typological connections early on. They saw that people, objects, and events in the Old Testament were *types* that foreshadowed a fulfillment in the New Testament, which are called *anti-types*.

We can appreciate these in books like the *Biblia Pauperum* (The Poor Man's Bible) and *Speculum Humanae Salvationis* (The Mirror of Salvation), which I heavily relied on to make sense of some titles in the Litany.

These books are collections of woodblock prints that put Old Testament types side-by-side with their New Testament anti-types. The juxtaposed pictures were a way to instruct "poor men and women" who couldn't read. Through prints like this, it is remarkable to see Mary foreshadowed; and it naturally excites me to share them with you.

I restrained from including doctrine for as much as I could, but it was just impossible to explain some of Our Lady's titles without so doing. In the end, the finished work is a marriage of Marian devotion, Catholic doctrine, and Old Testament typology.

Joby Provido
Easter 2018

INTRODUCTION

STORYTELLERS HELP THEIR AUDIENCE get to know the characters in their narratives better by using a literary device called *epithets*. These are descriptive phrases that express a particular quality of the person. *Achilles of the swift feet*, for example, alludes to his agility in combat. Romeo and Juliet are *star-crossed-lovers*. Smaug is the *worm of dread*. Batman is the *Dark Knight*. Harry Potter is *the boy who lived*. Daenerys Targaryen is *the unburnt, mother of dragons*. Even if we are not familiar with these characters, we get an idea of who they are from their appellations.

We have also attached nicknames to real people based on how we remember them best: Richard the Lion-Hearted, Jack the Ripper, Honest Abe Lincoln, Elvis the King of Rock and Roll, Winston Churchill the British bulldog, Mother Theresa – saint of the gutters.

Since Sacred Scripture is a story of God's love for us, we can also see God using epithets to help his chosen people identify who his promised Messiah was going to be. Through the prophets, he gave identifying marks that would identify Christ. When Daniel calls the Messiah *Son of Man*, for example, we understand Christ to be human. When Isaiah says the Messiah will be named *Emmanuel* (*God with us*), he indicates Christ's divinity. But when John the Baptist refers to Christ as the *Lamb of God*, it might not be apparent to us today what that is.

Some Christians think this title refers to how Christ meekly went to his death. While that may be true, to a first-century Jew the reference is quite clear. See, during those days, when one wanted to be forgiven of sins, the penitent would bring a sin offering – usually a lamb – to the temple. There a priest would slay it, spill its blood on the ground, and put the carcass on a pyre, so its aromatic roasting fat rises to heaven in prayer. With this in context, the title

Lamb of God acquires a richer meaning to indicate Christ is the victim that God gave humankind, whose blood will be spilled for the expiation of sins.

While Scripture does this to help us know Christ better, the Church, likewise, sheds light on who Mary is by giving her epithets in the form of titles. Sadly, as culture and language evolved, some of these titles also lost their context and meaning to the point of becoming so obscure that we don't know what they refer to today.

This is a tragedy because it is a missed opportunity to know Our Lady who, as queen and mother, loves each of us genuinely. We can't love someone whom we don't know, so if we don't know Mary, how can we return her affections? We also miss the chance to recognize what virtues the Church admires in her. So how can we imitate her love for God if we don't know what these good qualities are?

One way to know more about Mary is to understand her epithets, and that's one of the things this book can do. When her titles are given context, just like what we did for the *Lamb of God*, they gain a richer texture so we can appreciate Our Lady the way the Church originally presents her.

But, one might ask, how do we know her titles tell the truth about her? Aren't some titles just exaggerated expressions of devotion? The answer is no, at least not the titles in the Litany.

There is a saying in the Church, "Lex orandi, lex credendi"[1] that idiomatically translates to "what we say in prayer reflects what we believe." It should be no surprise that prayers distributed or said in public must have Church approval first.

The *Litany of the Blessed Virgin Mary* is one such example as it is said after the mysteries of the Rosary in private or in community prayer. On 11 July 1587, Pope Sixtus V issued a formal approval of the litany through a *Bull Reddituri* [2] that allowed it to be used publicly. This pronouncement would necessarily indicate that the titles of

---

[1] St. Prosper of Aquitaine, Eighth Book on Authority of Bishops. "Let us consider the sacraments of priestly prayers, which having been handed down by the apostles are celebrated uniformly throughout the whole world and in every Catholic Church so that the law of praying might establish the law of believing." Patrologia Latina, 55, pp209-210

[2] A bull is a papal decree that had a seal (bulla) of authentication.

4

Our Lady in the litany are recognized as accurately describing Mary's qualities without contradicting doctrine.

A Short History

Technically a *litany* is a series of short invocations. We can trace it so far back in Church history that we can say it is an integral part of Christian prayer. Today we commonly experience it at mass, and in the Liturgy of the Hours.

Litanies can be directed to God. For example, "Lord have mercy. Christ have mercy." They can be directed to different saints. The *Litany of the Saints*, for example, includes supplications to the three archangels, St. John the Baptist, St. Joseph, St. Peter, St. Paul, etcetera; to whom we ask to "pray for us."

A litany can also be dedicated to a particular saint. For example, the *Litany of the Blessed Virgin Mary* is one where we invoke Mary using her different titles. Its other, older, name is the *Litany of Loreto*.

Where did the Litany of Loreto come from? Unfortunately, the history of the litany is a cloudy one. The lack of documentation does not allow us to determine an exact year or place of its origin. The oldest known copy is the one found in Dillingen, Bavaria, Germany, which scholars believe to have existed as early as 1558. The title of this copy is in German, translated as *Litany of Loreto. Order of the Litany of Our Lady as said every Saturday at Loreto.* Although the official title of the manuscript implies that the Litany was said each Saturday in Loreto, Italy, it is difficult to conclude with confidence that that was the origin of the litany.

The title coincides nicely with the prayer book by Fr. Lovasik that I mentioned in the preface, which suggests each of Our Lady's titles is honored on Saturdays. However, the fact that the Dillingen document is a copy suggests it was based on some earlier printing – a manuscript we have no information about. Because we cannot find anything earlier, we will focus on the titles from the Dillingen text for that is the oldest version we have.

This book will examine and incorporate the older meanings of the titles to understand what it is the Church was ascribing to Mary at the time of the writing. The Litany was not originally in English but Latin. It also isn't known when the Litany was translated into English, but a translation must have been done after its approval so it could be circulated to the English-speaking world among others.

The words of some of the English titles in the Litany have lost their meaning as the usage changed through time. What might have meant something in the 16th century might no longer apply today. The word "amiable," for example, means "friendly" as we use it today. Its use has declined since the 1800s and originally meant "loveable." When we apply this to *Mater Amabilis*, for example, it makes more sense rendered as "Mother Most Loveable" as compared to "Mother Most Friendly.'

Another word that fails to translate the correct meaning of the Latin is *Mater Admirabilis* (*Mother Most Admirable.*) Whereas admirable means "delightful" in today's vernacular, the outdated meaning of admirable meant "wonderful." In fact, the Dillingen copy used "mirabilis" instead of "admirabilis" to indicate someone who possessed remarkable properties.

The Dillingen copy also used *Mater Piissima* (*Mother Most Devout* or *pious*, or *loving* or *dutiful*) while later versions changed this to *Mater Purisima* (*Mother Most Pure.*) It isn't clear why the change was made. Some sources think the meaning of *Piissima* was so vague that a more precise title was needed. Some others think that the letterforms are so similar to *Purisima* that it could have been a typographical mistake at some point. Both make sense, but the current rendering of *Mother Most Pure* seems more apt as it starts a group of titles that extols her purity.

In 1760 Augsburg, Germany, Joseph Sebastian Klauber rendered the litany as allegorical images using print engravings. It is worth noting that these carved print blocks already use the current form of *Mater Admirabilis* and *Mater Purisima.* It means that the changes were made in the 200 years between the Dillingen version and the Klauber engravings.

The Klauber engravings end with *Regina Sanctorum Omnium* (*Queen of All Saints.*) Since then, other titles have been added after it or within. The Dominicans, for example, included *Regina Sacratissimi Rosarii* (*Queen of the Holy Rosary*), which they printed in their Breviary in 1614. Pope Leo XIII later approved its use on December of 1883.[3]

Several places also added titles. For example, Venice used *Mater Veri Consilii* (*Mother of True Counsel*); Spain used *Mater Intemerata* (*Mother Undefiled*), as well as *Mater Immaculata* (*Mother Immaculate*). These titles were eventually officially added by virtue of Church approval. Pope Leo XIII added the former in 1903 as *Mater Boni Consilii* (*Mother of Good Counsel*), and *Mater Immaculata* was rendered as *Regina sine labe originali concepta* (*Queen conceived without original sin*) when Pope Pius IX defined the dogma of the Immaculate Conception in 1854. What is remarkable is that it was already included in the Litany in 1846 – an excellent example of how belief is not a result of dogma, but the other way around.

The other titles that were added to the Dillingen version were *Regina Pacis* (*Queen of Peace*) by Pope Benedict XV in 1927, *Regina in Caelum Assumpta* (*Queen Assumed into Heaven*) by Pope Pius XII in 1950, and *Regina familiae* (*Queen of Families*) by St. Pope John Paul II in December 1995.

How the Litany is Organized

The litany is grouped into major classifications of Our Lady's attributes. The first praises her holiness from *Holy Mary* to *Holy Virgin of Virgins,*

The next group refers to her as "mother" starting from *Mother of Christ* to *Mother of Our Savior*. Within that is a series that venerates her purity: *Mother Most Pure,* to *Mother Undefiled.* The other titles in this group describe her using the maternal qualities we admire in her.

The third group exalts her virginity from *Virgin Most Prudent* to *Virgin Most Faithful.*

The fourth group is composed of *types* (symbols) of Mary mostly foreshadowed in the Old Testament.

The fifth group praises her as our advocate in our physical and spiritual needs. These are from *Health of the Sick,* to *Help of Christians.*

---

[3] Sullivan, John F. The Externals of the Catholic Church. P.J. & Sons. 1918 pp 273-79

The last group refers to her as queen. This starts from *Queen of Angels* to *Queen of Peace*. A sub-grouping within honors her as Queen of the different types of saints from *Queen of Martyrs* to *Queen of All Saints*.

What the Litany Does

We fall in love with Our Lady. We learn about Mary through her titles because they point to the qualities that we revere in her. By prayerfully reflecting on these titles, we get a better appreciation of what we believe of Mary. As a result, we would like to know her more intimately through prayer and meditation of the mysteries of the rosary.

We give joy to Mary. For Catholics, Mary is our Queen, our Mother, and our intercessor; but far more fundamental than that, she is a woman – and what woman (or man) does not like to hear the good things about her? The titles of the litany highlight her different attributes. So instead of just saying "Mary, pray for us" several times, we use titles that point out her exemplary qualities. Just as a bride is thrilled when her husband calls her "dear, sweetheart, or honey," Our Blessed Mother is elated when we call her with our sweet-nothings too.

We honor Mary, and delight Jesus. Since Jesus gave Mary to us as our mother, we affectionately observe the fourth commandment by honoring her through her titles. Several personal revelations of Jesus to saints record him asking them to honor Mary. To Saint Margaret of Cortona, Jesus said, "Honor my mother, of whose beauty and greatness neither the world nor Scripture has spoken fully." To Saint Gertrude, he said, "I will repay you [for the honor]... you have shown my most sweet mother." To Saint Bridgette of Sweden, he also said, "Honor my mother as your Lady!" These are just a few, and it wouldn't be difficult to conclude that Christ delights in the honor we give his mother – his greatest creation.

It would be nice to honor Mary each Saturday as they did in Loreto. We can do this by saying the Hail Holy Queen, reading one title in the book, meditating on how we can integrate in our life the virtues honored in that title, praying the holy rosary (or part of it), and making and act of consecration to her. There are 51 titles in the Litany, so at the end of one year, we would have honored her each week.

We get to know Christ. As with most of Mary's titles and dogmas, they are not for her benefit, but to shine a light on the identity of Christ and the Paschal Mystery of our salvation of which they are both an integral part. Mary is a perfect reflection of her son. The titles, therefore, are understood in the context of Christ, which we are then drawn to contemplate. We are hard-wired to be attracted to the good, the beautiful, and to love. Therefore, as we contemplate Christ, we cannot but fall deeper and deeper in love with him for God is all good, all beautiful, and all loving.

The Titles of Our Lady
in the Litany

Holy Mary

TO BE HOLY MEANS TO BE DEDICATED TO GOD. It also means, *reserved formally for a divine purpose.* Mary is holy in both senses of the word.

"Holiness," as Blessed John Henry Newman explained is, "all that is most opposite and contrary to sin and guilt."[4] Therefore, when we say Mary is *holy*, we declare that there is nothing contrary to God in her – she is dedicated entirely to him. This means everything she does is in perfect union with God's will.

The gospel of Luke tells us that God sent the Angel Gabriel to Mary. His task was to invite her to become the mother of the Messiah.[5] We have to remember that Mary, at the time of this invitation, was already betrothed to Joseph. In the culture of first-century Jews, this meant that they were as good as married. The only remaining thing left to do was for Joseph to take her home so they could live together. Thus, we can consider Mary already as the wife of Joseph at this point.[6]

If Mary accepted this invitation, her pregnancy would be evident in a few months. This would pose a potential problem for her because this was not the child of her husband. We say this is a concern because she didn't know what Joseph's reaction might be. It is a possibility that he might brand her as an adulterer. If so, her life is in jeopardy because the punishment for adultery is stoning to death.[7]

---

[4] Newman, Bl. John Henry. *Meditations and Devotions.* Green, and Co. 1907
[5] Luke 1:26-33
[6] Sheed, Frank J. *To Know Christ Jesus.* Sheed & Ward. 1962
[7] C. Ceuppens, *De Mariologia Biblica*, Turin, 1951, p. 57;
     Strack, H. and Billerbeck, K.. *Kom mentarzum Neuen Testamentaus Talmud und Midrash*, vol. 2

Scripture is silent about what she told Joseph if anything at all. Scholars like to think she didn't discuss it with Joseph because she felt it was not for her to divulge what God had told her[8] – at least not before he was given instructions in a dream. So at the time when Gabriel was waiting for her answer, her consent would come at the price of an unclear – maybe dangerous – future.

Despite the risk, her resolution was, "Behold, I am the handmaid of the Lord. May it be done to me according to your word."[9] Her "fiat" (in Latin, "let it be done") is a testimony to her steadfastness to do God's will. It shows us that nothing can separate herself with what God wants of her even if it may mean a slow painful death by stoning. It also displays her trust in God's plan because without being given all the nitty-gritty details, she accepted whatever it was. We can better see this humility when we read her consent in the literal Greek translation, which is, "Behold I am the *slave* of the Lord..."

Before moving on, we need to understand the reaction of St. Joseph a little bit. Saint Matthew tells us that Joseph was a "just man" who didn't want to expose Mary, so he planned to divorce her. In a dream, an angel told him, "Joseph, Son of David, do not be afraid...give him the name 'Jesus'." Scholars have made beautiful sense of this juxtaposition of events. They suggest Joseph wanted to divorce Mary not because he thought she had an illicit relationship with another man; instead, he though he wasn't part of the plan so he didn't want to get in between God and Mary. That or he felt so undeserving to be part of God's plan that he wanted to be apart from it. He feared he was too insignificant – which is why the angel's words make perfect sense when he dispels that fear with, "do not be afraid."

In Jewish tradition, the giving of the name to a child during *brit milah* (covenant of circumcision) is an important one. It is a public acknowledgment that the one giving the name is the father of the one receiving the name. Prophets foretold that the Messiah was to come from the line of David,[10] so when God asked Joseph to give the

---

8   Sheed, Frank, *To Know Christ Jesus*
9   Luke 1:38
10 Isaiah 11:1 for example

son of Mary a name, his lineage to David is essential. The angel makes that clear when he calls him "son of David." It is as if the angel was telling Joseph that he, just as Mary, is part of this unfolding plan of God.

The second sense of the word *holy* describes something or someone reserved for a divine purpose. In the *Protoevangelium of James*, a manuscript that depicts the life of Mary and Joseph before their betrothal, we learn that she served at the temple. This kind of service requires a vow of perpetual virginity: the person reserves herself, and her ability to procreate, for the service of God. We see this kind of commitment in the prophetess Ana, during the Presentation in the Temple,[11] where we learn she dedicated her life to service after her husband died.

In the case of Mary, she surrendered herself to God's purpose in a symbolic sense when she gave her life to his service in the temple. However, she also "reserved herself for God's purpose" in a very literal sense when she agreed to become the vessel for God's only Son – and to no one else. Her womb was made for that one purpose alone: a means for God to fulfill his plan for bringing into this world its savior. Because she was "reserved" for God's design in his plan to become human, this makes her *holy* as no other can be holy in the sense of the word.

When invoking this title, consider that: Mary is holy above all creatures because she dedicates herself entirely to God.

---

[11]   Luke 2:36-37

HOLY MOTHER OF GOD

WHEN THE HOLY SPIRIT OVERSHADOWED MARY, the Second Person of the Blessed Trinity assumed human nature in her womb without losing his divine nature. Since she gave birth to him, Mary, then, is the *Mother of God* because she is the mother of Jesus who is both God and man.

While this might be straightforward to us today, it wasn't always that way. The Church had to wrestle against strange ideas about the person and nature of Jesus over the years. One strange notion was that Mary could not have been the "Mother of God" because her human nature was not capable of creating something divine. But that is to misunderstand motherhood and the Incarnation.

A human father and mother contribute to the body (matter) when conceiving a baby, and God creates the soul (spirit.) Regardless of who provided the components, a woman gives birth to a person, not to the individual components. It is, therefore, strange to separate the components when expressing motherhood. So even if it was God who created the soul, we never say a woman is the mother of her child's body only. What we do acknowledge is that she is the mother of the entire person that has a body, a spirit, and a human nature.

Therefore, when Mary gave birth to Jesus, it would be unreasonable to conclude she gave birth just to his human nature. Since mothers don't give birth to component parts, she must have given birth to a whole person that has a body, a spirit, a human nature, and a divine nature.

Sometime in the fifth century, a man by the name of Nestorius contested the title "Mother of God" (which necessarily means that the Church was already using this title). His reason was another strange notion that claimed there were two persons in Jesus: one human, and one divine. In his line of thinking, Mary gave birth to the human person only.

This idea is problematic because we believe that the two natures of God and man came together in one person and one *hypostasis*.[12] Because of the confusion Nestorius was causing, the Church had to give an official teaching on the matter. In the form of a dogma, the Church declared that Mary gave birth to a single person, Jesus, who has two distinct natures: human and divine. Because of this, the Church teaches, we can call Mary, *Mother of God*. It does not mean Mary is a goddess, that she created God, or that she came before God. It is a simple declaration that Jesus is divine.

This dogma safeguards the nature and identity of Jesus. It is like a moat and wall that protect a castle. Enemies will have to overcome the moat and scale the wall before attacking the castle within. Likewise, people with heretical ideas about Jesus are forced to wrestle with this and other Marian dogmas before they can harm what we believe of Christ's identity and nature.

Because Jesus is part of the Blessed Trinity, Mary's motherhood to Jesus creates a relationship with the other persons of the Trinity no one else has. She shares the right with the Father to call Jesus, "my son and yours." By being Christ's mother, she is associated with his mission to redeem and sanctify the world. Because the Holy Spirit overshadowed her,[13] she has the right to be called the *Immaculate Bride of the Holy Spirit*.[14] These are very personal relationships to God none of the angels and the rest of humanity can ever have!

When invoking this title, consider that: Mary is the mother of Jesus who is divine, and this gives her a special relationship with all the persons of the Blessed Trinity.

---

[12] Council of Chalcedon, 451
[13] Luke 1:35
[14] Pope Pius XII. *Address to Women of Italian Catholic Action,* July 13,1958; Lovasik, Lawrence. *Our Lady in Catholic Life,* McMillan Company NY. 1957

HOLY VIRGIN OF VIRGINS

THE TITLE REFERS TO THE DOGMA OF MARY'S PERPETUAL VIRGINITY that extols Mary's purity both physically and spiritually. It is an expression that Mary's elevated state of purity is high above the virginity of others.

The promise of the Messiah was always foretold as the "son of a woman."[15] Many generations after Adam and Eve, God spoke through the prophet Isaiah to reiterate this promise, "Therefore the Lord himself will give you a sign; a virgin, pregnant and about to bear a son, shall name him Emmanuel."[16] Throughout human history, God prepared humankind for the time he would unfurl his plan of redemption. "At the fullness of time,"[17] he sent the Angel Gabriel to a virgin in Nazareth to ask her if she would accept to be this woman. We have to remember that God and angels are spirits who don't use words to communicate with each other, so the angel Gabriel himself exquisitely crafted the words he used in the Annunciation.[18]

Mary was perplexed and asked, "How can this happen to me?" This speaks volumes about what is in her mind because one shouldn't wonder how a woman is to conceive considering she was betrothed to Joseph. This can only mean she was not considering any sexual relations with Joseph even from the beginning. And so the Angel Gabriel made it clear that the Holy Spirit will "overshadow" her.

Saint Matthew has a poetic way of showing this virginal conception. At the start of his Gospel, he lists down the genealogy

---

[15] Genesis 3:15
[16] Isaiah 7:14
[17] Galatians 4:4-7
[18] Sheed, Frank J. *To Know Christ Jesus*

of Jesus where he traces the father of each person. "Abraham became the father of Isaac, Isaac, the father of Jacob, Jacob the father of Judah," etcetera. This goes on for several generations, but when he gets to Joseph, he writes, "Jacob the father of Joseph, the husband of Mary. Of her was born Jesus who is called the Messiah."[19] He does not say Joseph is the father of Jesus but mentions only the mother. This fulfills all prophecies concerning the Messiah because they always mention the mother or the "woman" but never the father.

We should find this unusual because the Jewish culture of that time was very patriarchal. A son bore the name of his father. Saint Peter's name, for example, is Simon bar Jonah, which means "Simon, son of Jonah." Christ himself uses this in Matthew 16:17, "Blessed are you, Simon son of Jonah..." So not mentioning the father of the Messiah is insulting to the father. But maybe there is a better explanation: the plain truth is the Messiah has no human father. This, in fact, is the mystery of the virgin birth of Jesus because he was conceived without the participation of a human father.

The father is essential in Hebrew / Jewish culture because ancestry is traced through the fathers.[20] The Messiah, prophets said, would be a king who would come from the royal line of David.[21] This is a problem because Jesus has no paternal ancestry so how can he be a legitimate king of royal blood? The answer is in his naming.

An angel instructed Joseph to name Mary's son, "Jesus," [22] and he accomplished this during circumcision.[23] In Jewish custom when a man claims to be the father of a child that is not his, it is not a token gesture; on the contrary, the child becomes a true son or daughter of the man to the extent of inheriting his entire genealogy. In Hebrew, the rite of circumcision is called, "covenant of circumcision." In a covenant, one person gives himself (or herself) to another, and vice versa. An unbreakable relationship is formed! Therefore, when Joseph gave Jesus a name, he gave himself to Jesus

---

[19]   Matthew 1
[20]   Matthew chapter 1 for example
[21]   Isaiah 11:1 for example
[22]   Matthew 1:21
[23]   Luke 2:21

as a father, and Jesus gave himself to Joseph as a son. In this way, Joseph gave Jesus his royal lineage in a very real way. This is why Jesus' lineage can be traced back to Abraham in the Gospel of Matthew, or even to Adam in the Gospel of Luke – all because Joseph made him his son by simply giving him a name.

The way Jesus was brought into the lineage of David is the same pattern from which we understand our spiritual regeneration too. Baptism is the new circumcision, so through baptism, we become children of God.[24] Just as Joseph adopted Jesus when he named him, we become adopted children of God through baptism when we are given a name. So when the minister of Baptism gives us a name, it is "in the name of the Father, and of the Son, and of the Holy Spirit." The minister is acting *in persona Christi capitis* – in the person of Christ the head. It is like God "giving us a name" so that he gives himself to us as a father, and we give ourselves to him as children who inherit his divine life. Is it not what God had always desired when he said, "You will be my people, and I will be your God."[25]

Because Mary is *holy* in the sense that she is reserved for God alone, (see *Holy Mother of God*) her womb is not to be used for regular childbearing. If sacred vessels of the temple were not used for mundane things, how can the vessel that held God itself be used for anything else? (See also *Gate of Heaven*)

When we say Mary's virginity is perpetual, it means she was a virgin from the start of her life and thereafter for all eternity. Not even the birth of Christ injured her virginity. Artistic renditions of this idea use three stars: one on her left shoulder, one above her forehead, and one on her right shoulder. These symbolize her virginity before, during, and after the birth of Christ. (Sometimes, when images depict her carrying the child Jesus, and he covers and replaces one of the stars, the stars symbolize the Father, Son, and Holy Spirit.) Because Mary was chosen to be the Mother of God through a virgin birth, this elevates her above all virgins. Who else is a virgin that has given birth?

---

[24] Colossians 2:11-12
[25] Exodus 6:7

We may have gone through so many Christmases that we might take Christ's extraordinary birth for granted. We have to be amazed every time we think of it: imagine a child born without a human father. It is miraculous, and Mary is in the very center of it. She is the hinge between the Old and New Testament: how important is Our Lady!

When invoking this title, consider that: Mary is a virgin before, during, and after the birth of Christ.

MOTHER OF CHRIST

THE WORD CHRIST HAS ITS ORIGIN IN TWO WORDS: *Khriein* in Greek, which means, *anoint* and *Khristos*, which means *anointed one*. An anointing is done when a liquid – usually oil – is poured or smeared on a person or thing to indicate that he, she, or it is under the divine influence of God.

In the Old Testament, priests, prophets, and kings were anointed because they were said to have been chosen by God. The word *Messiah* also comes from the Hebrew verb *mashach*, and *Mashiach* that means *anoint*, and *anointed one* respectively. Thus, *Christ* and *Messiah* mean the same thing. Since the Messiah was believed to be sent by God to deliver Israel from foreign bondage, he was considered "anointed." This title of Mary identifies her son, Jesus, as the Messiah who is priest, prophet, and king. What does it mean to be these?

A priest, especially a High Priest, is the mediator of humankind to plead for God's graces and mercy. We see this in the person of Aaron, the first High Priest who had the exclusive right and responsibility to make offerings to God. Because the Israelites offended God by urging Aaron to fashion from gold an idol resembling the bull-shaped Egyptian god Apis, as High Priest he would slay a bull as a sacrificial victim to make amends for the people, as would every High Priest after him, on the Day of Atonement every year. Jesus is the High Priest who represents all of humankind when he offered himself as the sacrificial lamb on Good Friday – the definitive "Day of Atonement" that is eternally re-presented in every Holy Mass. The Gospel of John alludes to this when he describes one of the clothes of Jesus as a seamless tunic,[26]

---

[26]   John 19:23

which is the same type of vestment used by the High Priest on the Day of Atonement. Today, when our priest celebrates the Holy Sacrifice of the Mass, he wears an *alb* that represents the seamless tunic of Christ to remind us we are present in his sacrifice.

A prophet is someone chosen by God to reveal to his people some truth about himself. God either sends a messenger to the prophet or directly speaks to him. A prophet, then, is perceived as a teacher to guide God's people. Jesus came as a prophet when he revealed to us certain things about God that we could never know if it wasn't told to us. The Blessed Trinity is an example. He also taught us God's ways of understanding the Law – the commandments and instructions given by God to Moses. He also opened Scripture (the Old Testament at that time) to help us recognize that he is the Messiah the prophets have foreseen.[27] We get all these from the apostles whom Jesus taught day and night for almost three years. They would have learned not only from what he said but also from what he did, and how he did things. They saw him as a prophet, and we know this because when he performed the multiplication of loaves, the people said, "This is truly the Prophet, the one who is to come to this world."[28] We, also, shouldn't miss the fact that Christ was killed as every prophet was killed before him.

When the Angel Gabriel announced to Mary that she was chosen to be the mother of the Messiah, he said, "the Lord God will give him the throne of David his father..."[29] The words in themselves are an indication that God is choosing Jesus to be King. It is clearly an anointing. The kingdom of Christ is a spiritual one,[30] which we know as the Church fashioned after the Davidic Kingdom. It is a kingdom that is indefectible – has no end – as the Angel Gabriel promised: "and of his kingdom there will be no end."[31]

We acknowledge him as our high priest in every mass when the priest offers Christ (who represents us) to the Father as he says, "Through him, with him, in him, in the unity of the Holy Spirit, all

---

[27] Luke 24:13-35
[28] John 6:14
[29] Luke 1:32
[30] John 18:36
[31] Luke 1:33

glory and honor are yours, Almighty Father, forever and ever," and we raise our voice in consent, "Amen!" We acknowledge him as a prophet when we sit down beside him in prayer where we listen to him and learn from him in Scripture and from the Church that "extends his presence on earth."[32] We acknowledge him as king when we obey his commands to love one another, and to "do this in memory of me" in every mass.

If Jesus is the divine priest, prophet, and king, then there is nothing more important than to become his disciple for he has the words of eternal life.[33] Mary becomes our model in our pursuit of discipleship because she was in Calvary when Jesus, as priest and victim, offered himself to God in an eternal sacrifice. She is the first and model disciple of Christ with whom she had intimate conversations. Even before his public life, Mary was already learning from him. She was subjected entirely to Christ's will to share his Passion even if it meant pain and sorrow. It is for these reasons we say if we stay close to Mary, she will naturally lead us to her son.

When invoking this title, consider that: Mary is the mother of the foretold Messiah.

---

[32] CCC § 854
[33] John 6:60

MOTHER OF THE CHURCH

THE TITLE MOTHER OF THE CHURCH IS NOT NEW. There is evidence that Saint Ambrose used it as early as the 4th Century.[34] In 1964, at the close of the Second Vatican Council, Pope Paul VI formally declared Mary as "Mother of the Church." Later, in 1980, Saint Pope John Paul II inserted this invocation in the litany. More recently, on 3 March 2018, Pope Francis declared that the Universal Church would celebrate the Feast of *Mary, Mother of the Church* on the Monday following Pentecost.

There are two reasons why the Church gives Mary the title *Mother of the Church* even if she did not give birth to the Church. The first reason is that she nurtured the Church in its infancy.

No one disputes that Mary is the mother of Jesus. However as Christ hung on the cross, he gave his mother to the Church through the person of St. John. It is the chosen Gospel for this feast that quotes Christ saying, "Woman, behold your son; son behold your mother."[35] The two of them did not think this was some figure of speech for Mary went home with John that very day.

God's speech is unlike ours. Because God's will changes things, whatever he says changes reality. When he told the paralyzed man, "you are forgiven," he is forgiven.[36] When he told people that a dead girl, "is not dead but sleeping," he takes her by the hand, and she arose.[37] When he said of the bread, "this is my body," and of the wine "this is my blood," they truly become his body and blood. Therefore, when Jesus told John, "behold your mother," it is as real

---

[34]   Rahner, Hugo. *Mater Ecclesia - Lobpreis der Kirche aus dem ersten Jahrtausend.* Einsiedeln/Köln 1944
[35]   John 19:25-31, *Redemptoris Mater* #47
[36]   Mark 2:5
[37]   Matthew 9:24-25

as the way his speech makes things real. Because John was the representative of the Church, Mary is the Mother of the Church simply because Christ said so.

The Gospel of John continues to tell us that a soldier pierced the side of Christ wherefrom blood and water flowed. All this imagery helps us see Calvary as a "New Eden." The fall of humankind happened in the Garden of Eden, while our redemption happened in Calvary, where there is a garden.[38] We have Jesus, whom St. Paul refers to as the "New Adam."[39] In Genesis, we read that God put Adam under a deep sleep, and from his side, God formed Eve to become Adam's bride.[40] Adam called Eve, "woman," so when Jesus called Mary "woman" it is no act of disrespect or condescension, but the recognition that she is the "New Eve."

The Church Fathers easily saw that the blood and water from the side of Christ (who was dead and rose again as if in a "deep sleep") as the formation of the Church.[41] It was like a gestating baby in a womb waiting to be born and take its first breath. Thus, the Church is just like Eve who was formed from the side of her bridegroom. And just as God breathed life into the nostrils of Adam,[42] so did the Holy Spirit – as a strong wind – blow life into the nostrils of the Church on Pentecost.[43] This is why Catholics say Pentecost is the birthday of the Church.

Continuing this analogy, just as a newborn needs a mother for it to develop, the infant Church needed a mother to nurture her and help it in its first wobbly baby steps. In Catholic small-"T" tradition, we say Mary was that mother. Because one becomes a mother after birth, it seems only right to celebrate Mary as Mother of the Church the day after the Church was born.

From the Book of Acts,[44] we read that Mary and the apostles prayed together. This did not happen by chance, of course. All of Israel expected a mighty warrior king to liberate them from their

---

[38] John 19:41
[39] 1 Corinthians 15:45
[40] Genesis 2:21-22
[41] CCC § 766
[42] Genesis 2:7
[43] Acts 2:2
[44] Acts 1 & 2

enemies, so to his disciples, Jesus could not possibly be this Messiah if he was dead. Christ's demise dashed all their hopes and dreams. All the apostles and disciples, except John, were hiding in some dark place somewhere from fear of being arrested as their leader was.

Mary stuck by the side of her son to the bitter end. It was Mary who held the faith; it was her faith that kept the Church alive from Good Friday to Easter Sunday. They would have seen in her a strength that none of them had. So she must have been the rallying point for the Church at that desperate time: not Peter whose faith was shattered, not Andrew, not James nor John, not any of the apostles. We shouldn't be surprised that Saturday is the day dedicated to Mary because it was on Black Saturday that she held the faith when the faith of the apostles waned. We can be only too happy that seeing the resurrected Christ restored their faith.

After the Ascension, we can imagine Mary being at the center of gatherings where stories are told. Peter had the last say concerning doctrine and administration, but whenever the apostles wanted to know more about Jesus before his public life, there was no other person they could have turned to except Mary. After all, she would be the person who would know Christ more than any other since the announcement of his birth. The Infancy Narratives of Matthew and Luke, for example, could have come from no other source than Mary who "pondered and kept all these things in her heart."[45]

With all of these, it isn't surprising that Mary would be praying with the apostles or be in their companionship. It is just natural she would be with them, and they would be with her. The idea that she was not with them is what is unthinkable, as it doesn't follow the overall pattern of her devotion to Christ and his Church.

The mission of the apostles was to go out and tell the world of the Good News. After all, the word "apostle" means "one who is sent." We can imagine they had good days and bad days. Hecklers disrupted Peter's first "homily" on Pentecost, for example. We picture Mary as the person who would be there to listen to their stories of joy, frustration, achievement, and failure. Her life was not

---

[45] Luke 2:51

one of comfort, so she had the practical and moral authority to tell them that being a follower of Christ doesn't necessarily mean he will remove their troubles. She would be there as someone whose unfaltering presence and words of encouragement kept them going. Who does all these things if not a mother?

Because she acted as a mother, the apostles would have treated her as such. If Mary were not all this, we would not probably have a Marian devotion today for if it didn't start from the apostles, it would not have started at all knowing how cautious the Church is in introducing foreign ideas.

Today, Mary continues to listen to us, her children, for we believe that she continues to exercise her maternal role in heaven.[46] Just as a good mother gives gifts to her children, Mary is the *Mediatrix* from where graces flow.[47] While she increased the biological life of Jesus with her milk, she increases our spiritual life with graces.

The second way Mary is Mother of the Church is that it is the mystical body of Christ. In the Old Testament, God always presented himself as a bridegroom to Israel his bride. "For your husband is your Maker," Isaiah proclaimed.[48] In the New Testament Christ also spoke of himself as the bridegroom[49] – the same God who allowed his side to be opened from where the Church, his bride, came from.

In Genesis, we read the description of marriage between Adam and Eve as being "one flesh."[50] This is why we say Christ and his bride, the Church, are "one flesh" that are inseparable from each other. Another image of this is Christ's allegory: "I am the vine, and you are the branches."[51] When you inspect a vine, one can't tell where the branch starts and the vine ends – it is almost impossible to tell them apart at some point. The one thing that is true though is that branches won't survive if they are cut from the vine.

---

[46] CCC § 975
[47] CCC § 969, *Lumen Gentium* 62
[48] Isaiah 54:5-8
[49] Matthew 9:15
[50] Genesis 2:24
[51] John 15:5

This brings us to the idea of the Church as being the Mystical Body of Christ. Jesus is the head, and the Church is his body as Saint Paul understood.[52] They are inseparable from one another so much that the Catechism refers to this union as "the whole Christ."[53] In layman's terms, Christ and the Church are one and the same. Saint Joan of Arc said it plainly: "About Jesus Christ and the Church, I simply know they're just one thing, and we shouldn't complicate the matter." Therefore, if Mary is the Mother of Christ, she must also be the Mother of the Church for it is Christ.

When invoking this title, consider that: Mary is our loving mother who will guide, nurture, and protect us who are her children.

---

[52] 1Corinthians 12:12-27
[53] CCC § 795

MOTHER OF DIVINE GRACE

T HE WORD GRACE COMES FROM THE WORD GRATIS, which means *free*. Since God made all of creation, which includes us, he does not owe us anything. Therefore our life, the material things we possess, our health, and every kind of blessing we have is something we do not deserve. To deserve something, one must have an accomplishment to merit it; but we could not have possibly accomplished anything before creation because we did not exist. So everything we have is a grace from God that we must be thankful for.

Aside from the gifts of existence and material things, God gives us certain spiritual graces to help our spiritual life: wisdom, understanding, counsel, fortitude, knowledge, piety, and fear of God. To humankind, God gave Adam and Eve *preternatural gifts* – gifts that do not belong to our nature by right, but not beyond our nature to possess – such as infused knowledge, freedom from sickness and death, and full control of the mind over the body.[54] The most important gift of all, however, is the supernatural gift of sanctifying grace. It is the indwelling of God so that we share his divinity. It is supernatural because it is above our nature to be "divine," but this is in fact what happens because God allows us to share in his divine life. This is not to be misconstrued that we will become gods ourselves; but that God lives in us, so there is an indwelling of peace and joy that only he can give.

Sadly, Adam and Eve lost these preternatural and supernatural gifts when they chose to separate themselves from God through disobedience. Since these gifts are not part of human nature, they cannot continue without the indwelling of God – the giver of the

---

[54] Trese, Leo. *The Faith Explained*. Fides Publishers.1965

gifts. The preternatural gifts are lost forever, and that is why we need to labor to reap knowledge. That is why we are vulnerable to sickness and death that corrupts our bodies. That is why we are inclined to sin when our body rebels against what our mind knows to be right. Thankfully, through God's mercy, baptism restores sanctifying grace. It is lost once more if we sin, and regained again through the sacrament of reconciliation.

In the case of Mary, she is the *Mother of Divine Grace* because, among all of God's creatures, she is "full of grace."[55] Before she was conceived, God designed her to be a worthy vessel for Jesus to be born from. God gave her the exclusive and special privilege of being exempt from the stain of original sin. She was like Eve in whom God dwelled from the moment of her conception: baptism was not needed for her to have sanctifying grace.

No other mother can claim to be the Mother of God. This Divine Motherhood is another grace only she is privileged to have. Since the stain of Original Sin did not corrupt her human nature, she did not have the inclination to sin,[56] so she remained sinless all her life. Whereas our weakened human nature is defenseless against death, it suffers corruption; Mary's is not, so she did not experience death the way we know it. She was justly rewarded at her Assumption when God took her body to heaven so it would not be corrupted. It shows what we could have experienced if Adam and Eve did not sin. Although this grace was lost, the death and resurrection of Christ shows what can happen to us at the end of time when the glorious bodies of the faithful will be reattached to their souls and live in the presence of God forever.[57]

Because Mary is Queen of Heaven this puts her high above the angels – making her the summit of all creation – another grace bestowed on her that no other creature of God can claim, not even the angels themselves whose nature is higher than that of humankind.

Mary is the *Mother of Divine Grace* in another sense, too. If God, who is the origin of all graces, came to this earth through

---

[55] Luke 1:28
[56] Lovasik, Lawrence. *Our Lady in Catholic Life.* p22
[57] CCC § 1005; 1022

Mary, then it wouldn't be difficult to understand why he would allow all graces merited by Jesus to be distributed through Mary too. She is the *Mediatrix of all Graces*, and in that sense, she is *Mother of Divine Grace*. (See *Tower of Ivory*)

When invoking this title, consider that: Mary who is "full of grace," gave birth to Jesus who is the divine grace of the Father to us.

MOTHER MOST PURE

PURITY HAS MANY FORMS. It can be the freedom of contamination, unmixed origin, perfect tuning, and freedom from immorality. We say Mary is *Mother Most Pure* because we can find all these qualities in her.

The stain of Adam and Eve's sin is passed down to us from generation to generation. It was not originally part of human nature, but because of the disobedience by our first parents, our nature became tainted. Whereas we were not meant to be inclined to sin, because of this lack of grace, we are now vulnerable to concupiscence. We can then say we have a corrupt and adulterated nature. But, because of her Immaculate Conception, Mary is said to be free from this kind of contamination. She is most pure in this sense.

This makes Mary an example of God's original design of humankind: the prototype unpolluted by sin or stain of any sin. She is a model of what God had intended us to be. There is nothing in her that God did not intend.

Because Mary was gifted with sanctifying grace from the moment of her conception, the Holy Spirit dwelled inside her and had perfect influence over her. Not that she was a robot programmed to do God's will, but instead she was someone who chose to be subjected to the will of God. In her, there was no room for anything that wasn't God. So just like a pure sound that is impeccably in tune with other sounds, she is pure in this sense because she was in perfect harmony with God's will.

Sin is any disobedience to God. Mary was free of every imperfection – even the inclination to sin. This makes her pure because she is untainted by any personal immorality, even the lightest one.[58] She is our model of purity, virtue, and obedience to God's grace. She is the perfect example for the beatitude: "Blessed are the pure of heart for they shall see God."[59]

St. John Bosco said, "Holy Purity, the queen of virtues, the angelic virtue, is a jewel so precious that those who possess it become like the angels of God in heaven, even though clothed in mortal flesh." When we look at Mary, we can see her this way: a creature made of flesh, but pure like a holy angel.

When invoking this title, consider that: Mary is untainted by sin or any inclination to sin.

---

[58] Lovasik, Lawrence. *Our Lady in Catholic Life*. p245
[59] Matthew 5:8

MOTHER MOST CHASTE

CHASTITY – THE VIRTUE OF BEING CHASTE – refers to the absence of any sexual intention or activity. In reference to Mary, she is perfectly chaste in the sense that she had no intention of having sexual relations with anyone, not even Joseph; and that she remained a virgin her entire life. Chastity is the fruit of her purity, and since she is the *Mother Most Pure*, then she is also naturally *Mother Most Chaste*.

When the Angel Gabriel announced to Mary that she would have a child, she asked, "How can this be, since I have no relations with a man?"[60] In the title *Holy Mother of God*, we learned from the *Protoevangelium of James* that Mary took a vow of virginity. In the same manuscript, we also understand that the elders chose Joseph to be the "protector" of Mary. The way for him to do this was to marry her without necessarily having a child with her. From the title *Holy Virgin of Virgins* we noted that when Mary had to ask the Angel Gabriel how it was to happen that she would have a child, it meant that she had no plans of having a child conceived in the normal manner with Joseph or with anyone, immediately, or after that. Her vow of virginity was absolute. It was a perfect act of dedicating herself – consecrating herself – to God. (See *Holy Mary*)

The dogma of the perpetual virginity of Mary means she remained a virgin throughout her life. The chalice used during Holy Mass is not used for anything else. It is consecrated, so that is used only for a single purpose: to hold the blood of Christ. To use it for anything else or to disrespect it is a sacrilege. Mary was also created for a divine purpose, and that is to bear the Son of God. It

---

[60] Luke 1:34

would be a sacrilege for the womb that bore the Son of God to be used for anything else.

In the Old Testament, Ezekiel tells of a vision that foreshadows this: "The LORD said to me: This gate must remain closed; it must not be opened, and no one should come through it. Because the LORD, the God of Israel, came through it, it must remain closed."[61] One of the titles of Mary in the Litany of Loreto is *Gate of Heaven* (which we will explore later), and we can see how it connects beautifully with this phrase from the prophet. Her womb is a gate that is opened for God to pass through, and then it must remain shut.

The Sacred Tradition handed down to us that Jesus was her only child conforms to this prophecy. Mary had no other children except her "first-born" – a term that doesn't mean there was a second or third-born. Instead, it is a term used to refer to the child that "opened" the womb.

In the Jewish culture of that time, it should be the child next in line to take care of one's mother; it would be an insult not to do so. However, when Christ hung on the cross, he gave his mother to St. John, the apostle.[62] Jesus didn't have to do this if he had brothers or sisters to take care of his mother. This is why the Church Fathers saw the absurdity of Christ giving Mary to John if she had other children.

Her heart and mind were as chaste as her body so that others were always first in her life. When Joseph and Mary found the child Jesus in the temple, she said, "Your father and I have been looking for you with great anxiety."[63] Scholars of Scripture quickly point out that in the language she was speaking, the correct grammatical syntax should be, "I and your father..." Even in the rules of grammar, she could not put herself ahead of her husband.[64]

She was the mother of the divine Messiah, but she didn't think others ought to serve her. Instead, she downplayed all the glory and honor of that privilege and was a virtuous wife to Joseph. She made

---

[61] Ezekiel 44:1-2
[62] John 19:26-27
[63] Luke 2:48
[64] Sheed, Frank J. *Getting to Know Christ Jesus*

haste to the hills of Judah where she stayed for three months after she learned that her cousin, Elizabeth, was six months pregnant. That alludes Mary stayed until Elizabeth was full-term so she could help her until the birth of John the Baptist. At the wedding in Cana, she was quick to save the bride and bridegroom from embarrassment by ensuring the wine didn't run out. In the Passion of her son, she was beside him with total disregard to her disgrace and peril as the mother of a "criminal."

Even when she thought her role was over, she acceded to her son's request to be our Mother when he gave her to us from the cross – thus broadening the task God was asking her to do. For Mary, the love of God and neighbor always came first. Is it not proof of her charity – that she loved God with an undivided love; that she loved others before herself?

When invoking this title, consider that: Mary's great chastity prevented her from having any selfish cravings of the mind, heart, and body.

MOTHER INVIOLATE

B Y THE GRACE OF GOD, Mary is "ever virgin." She was created a virgin and remained a virgin – not even the birth of Christ violated her virginity. Because both her body and spirit were never violated, we call her *Mother Inviolate.*

In the Old Testament, there was a time when Midianites overpowered the Israelites. When it was time for the Israelites to harvest crops, without fail the Midianites would come in force and, like locusts, raided the land until it was "laid waste." Israel cried out to God, and he sent an angel to talk to a warrior named Gideon. The angel's opening words were, "The Lord is with you, you mighty man of valor!" Then the angel instructed Gideon on what to do to liberate themselves from their enemy.

To be entirely sure he wasn't just hallucinating, Gideon asked for proof of this foretold victory; he asked God to miraculously fill a woolen fleece with dew while the ground around it remained dry. To make a long story short, God gave him this sign, and when Gideon and his men went to battle, they sent the enemy running, captured the enemy kings, and thus freed themselves from the enemy.

The Church has seen this as a prefiguration of Mary's conception of Jesus. When the Angel Gabriel greeted her, it was, "Hail, Full of Grace, the Lord is with you!" – quite similar to that of Gideon. Mary, a devout Jew who knew Scripture, would have been reminded that Gideon, Moses, Joshua, and David[65] were all greeted similarly as a prelude to God asking them to do something for him. Therefore, it is sensible to imagine that Mary saw this greeting was leading up to something God was going to ask of her. This could be

---

[65] Exodus 3:12, Joshua 1:5, 2 Samuel 7:1-2

why Scripture tells us she was disturbed, not by the angel's appearance, but by his greeting.[66]

Indeed God was asking her to do something: to conceive the Messiah who would liberate the world from sin and death. Lumen Gentium tells us, "Christ's birth did not diminish his mother's virginal integrity but sanctified it."[67] Poetically put, "As the rays of the sun penetrate glass and yet do not break or injure it in any way, so Jesus, the Sun of Justice, was born of you without violating [your] virginity."[68] The overshadowing on her of the Holy Spirit was like that of Gideon's fleece: "heavenly dew" miraculously entered her womb without violating her just as heavenly dew entered the fleece without breaking it.[69]

Mary's miraculous conception of Jesus is a *sign* of our liberation just like the miracle of the fleece was the sign of Israel's liberation. This time it is no longer from the enemy of God's people, the Midianites, but liberty from the real enemy of God's people – the devil. His overpowering lies prevent humankind from escaping the attraction to sin. In our vulnerable state, he continually robs us of our innocence and good works until we are laid waste. Mary's miraculous conception of Christ is the fulfillment of the Psalm: "The Lord shall come down like rain upon the fleece"[70] that heralds the devil's defeat.

We also should not miss the Scriptural connection when Isaiah told King Ahaz that as a sign of liberation, a virgin would get pregnant and call him "Emmanuel" for this is the same imagery of a fleece miraculously being filled with dew, and for the same purpose: a sign of liberation from the attraction to sin, and from death.

Misleading us to sin is the devil's way of maliciously invading our body – the temple of the Holy Spirit – and consequently pushing God out of it. This forced entry is a spiritual violation of our souls! These brutal attacks wound us every time we sin. Even if we heal, we are full of scars that disfigure us, but God chooses to see through them. While we look worn out from battle, Mary's soul was

---

[66] Sheed, Frank J. *Getting to Know Christ Jesus*
[67] *Lumen Gentium* 57
[68] Lovasik, Lawrence. *Our Lady in Catholic Life.* p250
[69] *Biblia Pauperum.* Block A, p 99.
[70] Psalm 71:16

pristine from the moment of her conception and continues to remain unblemished forever without a single spot of sin.[71] Just as Mary's virginity was never violated, the enemy also could never violate her soul.

When invoking this title, consider that: Mary's virginity was never violated, and neither was her soul.

---

[71] CCC § 493; *Lumen Gentium*

MOTHER UNDEFILED

THE OLDER MEANING OF "TO BE DEFILED" is an idiomatic expression that means that the innocence of a woman has been breached. Because the marriage act is a beautiful thing, being "defiled" isn't a judgment against purity, but a classification of a woman's state of virginity.

We don't use this word today to describe this wonderful state of womanhood because of its derogatory connotation, but we have to work with it because it is used in this title of Our Lady. So in its older reference, every woman who has given birth, must have been at one time been "defiled." All women, that is, except Mary. Because she conceived without a human agent, she was never defiled.

When God first spoke to Moses, it was under the appearance of a burning bush that wasn't consumed. To show this visually, great artists have always rendered the bush with green leaves, but on fire. It is a foreshadowing of the integrity of Mary's purity. If God, as fire, can inhabit a bush without it losing its freshness and greenness, so can God inhabit Mary without losing her virginity.[72]

Another way a woman can be "defiled" is through childbirth. However, the dogma of Mary's Perpetual Virginity declares that childbirth did not breach Mary's virginity as well. Through her Immaculate Conception, Mary was free of the sad effects of original sin.[73] One of these effects is pain during childbirth. "To the woman, God said: I will intensify your toil in childbearing; in pain you shall bring forth children..."[74] However, this does not apply to Mary for

---

[72] *Biblia Pauperum*: Nativity. Block B. p100.
[73] CCC § 418 "As a result of original sin, human nature is weakened in its powers, subject to ignorance, suffering and the domination of death, and inclined to sin (this inclination is called 'concupiscence')"
[74] Genesis 3:16

she is a "new creature."[75] So when Mary gave birth to Jesus, she was exempted from labor pain, and her virginity was kept intact. She is undefiled in this sense too.

Christ explained to his disciples that "evil thoughts, unchastity, theft, murder, adultery, greed, malice, deceit, licentiousness, envy, blasphemy, arrogance, and folly," are what can defile a person.[76] So when we ascribe to Mary that she is undefiled, we are saying she had none of these. This is because Mary was spared from the other effects of original sin too such as disease of the body, rebellion of the body against the will, and ignorance.

Blessed John Henry Newman expressed holiness as, "the absence of whatever sullies, dims, and degrades a rational nature..." Since Mary is Holy (See *Holy Mary*), there is nothing of these that desecrates her or her human nature. "For," continues Newman, "He [God] began, not by giving her the gift of love, or truthfulness, or gentleness, or devotion, though according to the occasion she had them all. But he began his great work before she was born; before she could think, speak, or act, by making her holy, and thereby, while on earth, a citizen of heaven. Nothing of the deformity of sin was ever hers."[77] How can it not be fitting for God to do this for her if she was going to be the Mother of God?

While her mind was never defiled, so was her body. Because she never sinned, this meant her body was undamaged both in substance and in appearance. Hers was a body that was in perfect harmony with her will without an iota of sinful desire whatsoever. Unlike the darkened minds we have, her mind was so enlightened that her judgments were sound. In this sense, too, her body was undefiled.

Since death is a result of original sin, and she was prevented from taking part in it, death and its effects could not touch her. At the end of her life, God assumed (took up) both her body and soul without her body suffering any corruption. Even death could not defile her body!

---

[75] CCC § 493; *Lumen Gentium*
[76] Mark 7:20-23
[77] Newman, Bl. John Henry. *Meditations and Devotions*

When invoking this title, consider that: Mary's body and soul were never corrupted in any way.

MOTHER MOST AMIABLE

THE LATIN TITLE IS MATER AMABILIS and was translated into English as *amiable*. Through the years, the use of the word *amiable* has evolved. Today we understand it to mean *friendly, pleasant,* or *agreeable.* However, the earlier use of the word is *loveable* from the Latin word *amare,* and *lovely* from the Latin word *amabilis.* So in this title, we are to apply it to Mary as *Mother, most loveable.*

Spiritual beauty is so loveable to God's eyes. The spiritual perfection of Mary was so attractive to God that she became the object of the Blessed Trinity's most tender love that hasn't been expressed to any other creature. The Father loved Mary so much that he allowed her to be the Mother of his only Son. In this way, he firmly united her to his saving plan for humankind.

The Son showed his love for Mary by being subjected to her for thirty years.[78] When it was time for him to step out of his "hidden life," it was through a spectacular miracle of turning water into wine in Cana at her suggestion. One of the last acts of the Son was to show love to Mary when he provided for her by giving her to the care of St. John.

We are consistently called to be other Christs. If Christ, Our Lord, and God, loved his mother so much, how can we say we are another Christ if we don't love Mary?

The idea of Mary, in God's mind, must have been so loveable that the Holy Spirit foretold of her coming by enlightening the prophets generations before she was conceived. She is like a song in God's mind whose chorus repeats time and time again on the lips of his spokesmen, the prophets.

---

[78] Luke 2:51

While we enjoy the indwelling of the Holy Spirit only from the moment of our baptism, the Holy Spirit showed how much he loved Mary by dwelling in her from the moment of her conception. He could not allow the devil to have dominion over her, so he protected her from sin throughout her whole life. This purity makes Mary so loveable in the eyes of God.

In the Old Testament, the Book Song of Songs allows us to eavesdrop on a bridegroom and his bride as they remark, in lyrical fashion, how much they love each other. It is an allegory for God and his bride, Israel. However, the Holy Spirit is such a master of language the he inspired writers of Scripture to use words that can contain many levels of meaning. It is because of this we can perceive Mary as the personification of Israel too. (See *Mother Most Admirable*) Later, we will also see how it can be a love story between Christ and his Church. (See *Tower of David*, and *Tower of Ivory*.)

So in the Song of Songs, we can put words into the lips of God speaking to Mary when the bridegroom says, "How beautiful is your love, my sister, my bride... You have ravished my heart with one glance of your eyes."[79]

The Father loves the Son because the Son is the perfect expression of the Father. Mary, on the other hand, is the perfect reflection of God's beauty. From all eternity, God saw this so we can understand why he loves her so much.

Since God is love itself, we are drawn to love him. Because Mary is the perfect reflection of God's love, we, too, are drawn to love her – she who possesses this virtue of her son more than anyone else does. How can we not fall in love with her too, she who is God's most perfect reflection?

When invoking this title, consider that: Mary's spiritual perfection is so beautiful that God loves her above all of creation.

---

[79] Song of Songs 4:9-10. There is no allusion to incest in the words, "my sister, my bride." They are just expressions of closeness that don't necessarily state a familial relationship.

MOTHER MOST ADMIRABLE

THE OLD TESTAMENT CONSISTENTLY FORETOLD that the Messiah would be born of Israel.[80] We can also read, in the Old Testament, how God consistently expressed his delight for his unblemished bride, "Daughter of Zion" [81] (or "Zion" for short.) Since the Messiah was born of Mary, early Christians equate Mary as the new Zion.[82] With this, it shouldn't be difficult to see how they saw that Mary is delightful to God.

The word *admirable* connotes respect or approval, but it also means *to look with delight*. It is easy to appreciate, then, in one sense that *Mother Most Admirable*, means *Mother Most Delightful* in God's eyes.

When Isaiah prophesied about Zion, he described a "Builder" marrying a virgin. He proclaimed, "For as a young man marries a virgin, your Builder shall marry you."[83] Although "Builder" pertains to God in this verse for he is the one who created Zion and the entire universe, it is a clever use of the word because the Greek word to describe Joseph in the New Testament is not "carpenter" but *tekton* or "builder."[84] It isn't difficult to see how both Zion and Mary fit this prophecy.

Isaiah continues to say, in the same chapter, that God is delighted with his bride and gives her a new name. This name articulates how he feels about her; and by extension, Mary. The Lord says, "But you shall be called 'My Delight is in her'."[85]

---

[80] Zephaniah 3:14-17, Micah 4:10, Isaiah 26:17-19; 66:6-10
[81] EWTN, *Mary in Scripture*. Web.
http://www.ewtn.com/library/MARY/MARYINSC.HTM
[82] *Lumen Gentium*
[83] Isaiah 62:5
[84] Mark 6:3, Matthew 13:55
[85] Isaiah 62:4

Writers of the New Testament confirm this notion too.[86] Jesus would often describe the Kingdom of God, the Church – the new Israel / Jerusalem – in terms of a wedding feast. It is still the same imagery of God as a bridegroom marrying his delightful bride.

We read in the Book of Revelation[87] that he is so excited to meet his bride, the New Jerusalem – a city described so magnificently – he expresses how pleasing it is to him. Mary is also a symbol of the Church because she is the unblemished bride of the Holy Spirit. Therefore, the delight of God for his bride can also be applied to the Church.

While God sees Mary as delightful in this way, humankind sees her *admirable* in another sense. The word comes from two Latin words: *ad* (to) and *mirari* (marvel) loosely translated as, "to be wondered at." It expresses a sense of awe. From the perspective of humankind, Mary is indeed marvelous to the point of being awesome.

Going back to the Old Testament again, one of the humans that was given a vision of Mary was the prophet, Isaiah. It is he who says of Mary: "Behold a virgin shall conceive, and bear a son..."[88] When God allowed Isaiah to foresee Mary, Isaiah is so full of admiration that he uses the word "behold" as an expression of wonder and awe. Even Isaiah could not contain himself.

Because Christ had no human father, his flesh came solely from her flesh. Likewise, the blood that runs through his veins is her blood. He is, in a genetic sense, a "male Mary." We marvel at what kind of perfect body God created for her if she was to be the genetic source of Christ. We marvel at what God has done for her: becoming a mother and preserving her virginity. We marvel at her spiritual perfection for from the moment of her conception to the moment of her life's end, the Holy Spirit kept her away from sin and made her a fitting temple to dwell in. We marvel at her perfect consent to God's will for from the moment of the Annunciation, during the Passion, and until the end of her time on earth, she unwaveringly united herself to his plan of salvation.

---

[86] Acts 13:32, Hebrews 1:5, Revelation 7:4-8; 12:1-2; 21:12-14
[87] Revelation 21:9-27
[88] Isaiah 7:14

Arnold of Chartres said, "The wills of Christ and of Mary were then united so that both offered the same holocaust. In this way, she produced with him the one effect, the salvation of the world."[89] We marvel at no other creature as we do Mary; truly, she is "Our tainted nature's solitary boast."[90]

When invoking this title, consider that: Mary is such a delight to God and a marvel for us to behold.

[89] Liguori, St. Alphonsus, *The Glories of Mary*. Catholic Book Publication Co. Revised.1996
[90] Wordsworth, William. *The Virgin*

MOTHER OF GOOD COUNSEL

ONE WAY TO UNDERSTAND THIS TITLE is to see Mary as the one who gave birth to Jesus whom Isaiah said, "They name him Wonder-counselor."[91] However, we get a clue of what attribute of Mary the title intends to exalt through the mass readings on the *Feast of Our Lady of Good Counsel*. We find there; she is the personification of *wisdom*. (See *Seat of Wisdom*)

Before going to that, there is a fascinating story of why we commemorate this feast, and it is worth telling. In the small town of Genazzano, Italy, there was a small church dedicated to *Our Lady of Good Counsel*. Over time, the church fell into disrepair, and in 1467, a widow claimed to have been inspired by the Blessed Mother to rebuild it. She started the project but couldn't complete it with the very meager funds at her disposal. The townsfolk ridiculed her, but that didn't stop the elderly woman because she was buoyed by the confidence that the Blessed Virgin would finish the work herself.

In the meantime, Ottoman Turks invaded Albania across the sea. Since they devastated almost everything that was Christian, a well-known ancient icon of *Our Lady of Shkodra* was in danger of being destroyed in a church there. During the attack on the city, two local men stopped at the church praying for safety as they escaped the incoming Turks. Our Lady promised them the icon would not be desecrated and told them to go wherever the fresco would go. Then the image miraculously detached itself from the wall, was enveloped by a white translucent cloud, and hovered across the Adriatic Sea. The two men followed it by walking on the sea until they reached Italy where it disappeared from their sight.[92]

---

[91] Isaiah 9:5
[92] Horvat, Marian Therese. *The Valiant Woman, Petruccia, and the Image of Our Lady of Genazzano.*

On that same day, April 25, to celebrate the feast of St. Mark, the residents of Genezanno gathered in the town square where the church of *Our Lady of Good Counsel* was built. The luminous white cloud descended on them and played beautiful music until it stopped over the unfinished church. Then the bells of the tower began to ring on their own where it was later accompanied by other bells in the town. The cloud then dissipated and revealed that the fresco, it had been carrying, was now "transferred" to a wall in the church. The town rejoiced with the words, "A miracle! Long Live Mary, Our Mother of Good Counsel."[93]

When the two men from Albania heard of the miracle, they went to the church to see the icon of Shkodra in its new home. Soon after, there were numerous reports of miraculous healings, people converting, and prayers answered. This naturally attracted tourists that improved the economy of the town. That, in turn, provided funds to complete the endeavor of refurbishing the church. We should derive a lesson from this: the widow who listened to Mary's advice was not disappointed.

The image still baffles investigators today. A fresco is a watercolor mixed with wet plaster painted on a wall or ceiling, so it isn't like a painting you can take off a wall. Authority figures who scrutinized the image confirm that the icon is made of pigment on a porcelain layer whose thickness is as thin as an eggshell. How the image was transferred from one wall to another is impossible to comprehend. Furthermore, investigators also examined the church in Albania to find that the image that had been venerated for centuries was indeed missing – and in its place is an empty space with the exact dimensions of the icon now in Genazanno.

Since the church was under the Augustinians, they were the ones who spread the devotion and placed their order under her patronage during the Counterreformation. Because of the great acceptance of this devotion, it wasn't surprising that several popes like Benedict XIV, Pius VII, Pius IX, and Leo XIII joined the *Pious Union of Our Lady of Good Counsel*. The devotion is still alive today and etched in our liturgical calendar on April 26.

---

[93] *Ibid.*

However, what is it we attribute to Mary through this devotion? To *counsel* means to *advise*. When we ask counsel from someone, that person ponders, deliberates, and determines what to do in a specific situation. It is understandable that we seek advice from people we know have some attributes to guide us. These could be wisdom, knowledge, and experience, to name a few.

Because of Mary's Immaculate Concepcion, and being sinless her whole life, she has the qualities of being a good counselor. Sin clouds the mind, but because the stain of original sin was prevented from affecting Mary, her intellect was neither darkened nor clouded. Since she remained sinless, her mind remained lucid. Thus, her counsel is free from the slightest failure in thinking. Furthermore, the indwelling of the Holy Spirit from the moment of her conception filled her with his gifts – the foremost of which is wisdom. Therefore, when we ask Mary for guidance in anything grave or trivial, we can expect the wisest counsel we can get from any human.

Another attribute of Mary is that she is our mother too. What mother wouldn't want only the best for her children? Since we are under her maternal care, she will give us only advice that is good for us. Her counsel is something we can trust and have confidence in.

Since she is our mother, she also will not turn us away when we seek her counsel. There is no concern too big that we can bring to her loving attention. There is nothing too small to be unimportant to her if it concerns her children.

Prayer is how we ask for advice from Our Lady. Ordinarily, you do not expect a voice to answer unless you are a mystic. Her answer will most likely come in the form of an inspiration or resolution. Maybe an event will intervene in the natural course of things. However, we will need time in silence and prayer to discern what her answers are in the things happening around us.

As we grow in prayer, it is with utmost certainty we will hear her counsel, to the waiters in Cana that is meant for us too. This episode in Scripture is the purposefully selected Gospel reading for the *Feast of Our Lady of Good Counsel*, where, referring to her son, her advice was to, "do whatever he tells you."[94] In that occasion, her counsel was united to the will of her son. And if this is so, we can be assured that we will succeed if we heed her counsel for it involves the will of God.

The church recognizes the wisdom of Our Lady. This is evident when the Church chose the reading for the celebration of this feast to come from the wisdom Scriptures and put the words on Our Lady's lips, "I am the mother of fair love, and of fear, and of knowledge, and of hope. In me is all grace of the way and of the truth, in me is all hope of life and of virtue... He that listens to me shall not be confounded: and they that keep my ways, shall not sin. They that read my lessons aright shall have life everlasting."[95]

When invoking this title, consider that: heeding Mary's wise advice can bring only good things.

---

[94] John 2:5

[95] Ecclesiasticus 24:26-31 Douay-Rheims. (Sirach 24:17-22) "He who listens to me will never be disappointed. He who lives by me will do no wrong. He who reads my lesson aright will find eternal life."

MOTHER OF OUR CREATOR

MARY IS THE MOTHER OF JESUS, and because of this, she is the mother of our creator in two senses. In the first sense, she is the mother of the Person through whom all creation was made possible. We attribute creation *ex-nihilo* (from nothing) to the Father, but we profess in the Nicene Creed that in Jesus, "through him all things were made." Saint John writes: "All things came to be through him, and without him nothing came to be..."[96] St. Paul's reiterates this in his letter to the Colossians, and by our catechism.[97] Because Mary gave birth to the person from whom through all things came into being, that would make her the mother of our creator.

In the second sense, Mary is the mother of a "new creation" in a spiritual way when St. Matthew subtly discloses that Jesus is not a product of any human father.[98] Therefore, he is not like the former created humans, but the *firstborn* of a "new creation."[99]

The sin of Adam and Eve plunged humankind into the realm of spiritual death. Although man's body was living and breathing, his soul was "dead." By becoming man, through his death and resurrection, Christ was able to breathe new life into man's soul just as God breathed life into man's body in the original creation of Adam. "The second creation took place when the Son of God came down to earth to create the world anew and to make it more wonderful than it was in the beginning."[100]

---

[96] John 1:3
[97] Colossians 1:16, CCC § 291
[98] Matthew 1:16
[99] Pope Benedict XVI. *Jesus of Nazareth: The Infancy Narratives*. Image. 2012
[100] Lovasik, Lawrence. *Our Lady in Catholic Life*

Mary is instrumental in this new creation. Through her consent to be the mother of Jesus, she, in a sense, "gave a way" for God to accomplish his plans for a new creation where man's soul is brought to a life where grace abounds and where death has no venom. Because she is the mother of the person who *makes all things new*,[101] she can be called *Mother of our Creator*.

When invoking this title, consider that: Mary is the mother of Jesus through whom all creation, old and new, was made.

---

[101] 2 Corinthians 5:17, Revelation 21:5

MOTHER OF OUR SAVIOR

A SAVIOR IS SOMEONE WHO RESCUES OR LIBERATES another from danger or captivity. When, at the Garden of Eden, man spurned the friendship of God through disobedience, he separated himself from God and at the same time allowed himself to be enslaved by the devil. The Gospel of John says of the devil: "He was a murderer from the beginning and does not stand in truth, because there is no truth in him. When he tells a lie, he speaks in character, because he is a liar and the father of lies."[102]

God told Adam and Eve that if they ate the fruit of a tree that he forbade, they would die. However, the serpent suggested God lied when he said, "You certainly will not die!"[103] The serpent was the one who lied when he told them they would be like gods if they ate the forbidden fruit.[104]

Adam and Eve willingly fell for these lies. We say "willingly" because they were given the preternatural grace of infused knowledge.[105] That means they knew all there is to know about the natural universe because, as a gift from God, it was part of their minds when they were created. With this grace, they were not easily tricked by the serpent. Instead, they saw things very clearly and weighed things very well before they mistakenly decided that it was God who lied to them. They let their trust in God die in them – that is the definition of Original Sin and of every sin.[106]

If friendship is like a door, Adam and Eve walked out God's door and unknowingly entered the devil's realm. This diabolical dominion distorts truth, and right away, the effects manifested

---

[102] John 8:44
[103] Genesis 3:4
[104] Genesis 3:5
[105] Trese, Leo. *The Faith Explained.*
[106] CCC § 397

themselves. First, Adam and Eve have a distorted view of God: they hid from him because they thought he was something to be feared. It is a complete reversal of when they would walk with God in the garden in friendship and trust. Second, they also have a distorted view of each other: they covered themselves with loincloths because they realized they were naked – when they had been naked all along. In the enemy's dominion, humankind is like a prisoner because, without graces, we are in danger of repeatedly falling back into error through the enemy's lies. Worse than that, death has taken hold of mankind in its inescapable grasp. It was God, after all, who was telling the truth.

We were prisoners of sin and death, but Isaiah foresaw the coming of the Messiah who would free mankind when he says about him: "He has sent me to bring good news to the afflicted, to bind up the brokenhearted, to proclaim liberty to the captives, release to the prisoners."[107] At the start of his ministry, this is the verse that Jesus chose to read from Scripture in the synagogue and acknowledged that he is this liberator when he said, "Today this scripture passage is fulfilled in your hearing."[108]

God sought Mary's consent for him to use her womb, and she gave it. God sought Mary's consent to give him a human nature, and she gave it. Because of her consent, she set in motion God's plan to save the world by giving birth to the Messiah that would redeem humankind.

What is it mean to be a *redeemer* though? The story of Ruth, in the Old Testament, gives us a clue. During a terrible famine, the husband of a woman named Naomi died, leaving her to take care of their two sons. One son married a woman named Orpah; the other, a woman named Ruth. After ten years, both men also died, making widows all three women.

In the patriarchal culture of that time, widows were in a terrible predicament because it was the men that did business. Without a husband, a widow would most likely become financially ruined, especially if there were debts to be paid.

---

[107] Isaiah 61:1
[108] Luke 4:21

56

Knowing this, Naomi gave Orpah and Ruth their leave so they could find husbands. Orpah left, but Ruth was kind enough to stay and take care of her mother-in-law, Naomi.

Together they went to Bethlehem during the barley harvest. Ruth gathered grain in the field of a man named Boaz who happened to be a relative of Naomi. Boaz was kind to Ruth and gave her refuge by instructing others not to rebuke or harm her.

One night, at the instructions of Naomi, Ruth positioned herself at the feet of the sleeping Boaz. He felt compassion for her and revealed he was a *husband redeemer*. This meant he could put someone under his care, which would mean he would acquire her land and all her debt. It also meant he would be responsible for all those under her. This is exactly what Boaz did when he took over Naomi's property. He assumed her debt, he put Naomi under his care, and he married Ruth.

It isn't difficult to see how this story explains how Christ redeems us. When Adam and Eve disobeyed God, they incurred a debt neither they nor their children could ever pay. But God and Israel gave themselves to each other in an unbreakable covenant the way husband and wife give themselves to each other in marriage. Christ becomes the bridegroom of the Church who puts herself at his feet in service to him. All nations (lands) are put under his care.

That the story of Ruth's redemption takes place in Bethlehem where she first meets Boaz is no coincidence too; for it is in Bethlehem where we first meet Our Lord and redeemer, Jesus Christ.

The payment of the Adam and Eve's debt is death – the consequence of Original Sin. It isn't just any death, but the willingness to face a humiliating and painful death in obedience to God. This would reverse the disobedience of Adam and Eve who were told they would die if they ate of a certain fruit. So Christ was "made to be sin"[109] and through his death on the cross, he paid the debt we could not pay.

---

[109] 2 Corinthians 5:21

We proclaim in the Nicene Creed that, after his death, Christ descended to "the dead." In the Apostle's Creed, we say he "descended to hell," but we do not mean he went to the place of the damned where there is an eternal separation from God. Instead, we mean he went to *Sheol*, the abode of the dead. It is in this "place" good men were "detained" for they could not yet go to heaven for it was still closed to them. The claws of death could not keep dead the author of life because that would be inconsistent with God being life itself. Instead, Christ descended so he could "break down the doors" of Sheol and eventually usher these good men and women to heaven when he opened it in his Ascension. Is this not the fulfillment of when Samson broke the gates of Gaza when men tried to keep him in the city to kill him?[110]

Before the time of the kings, God sent judges to Israel. They were not magistrates who arbitrated on disputes. Instead, they were people who helped Israel against their enemies. When the Philistines lorded it over the Israelites, Samson rose up and fought against them. He burned their grain fields by tying torches to tails of three hundred jackals and setting them loose in their plantations. When he was brought to the Philistines to face justice for this deed, he single-handedly killed a thousand of them using just a jawbone of an ass.

It was natural that the Philistines wanted to get even with him, so they most likely sent out spies to learn his patterns and whereabouts. Once, Samson went into the city of Gaza and visited a prostitute. (It is interesting that Scripture would give us this scandalous detail, but to share with us the weaknesses of God's champions is proof of its authenticity.) Regardless, the Philistines knew he was in the city, and they set a trap for him. The plan was to have assassins keep watch at the gate and kill him when he tries to leave the city in the morning.

Gates were an essential piece of protection during those times because it could regulate whom you wanted to let in or out of the city. They could be closed to prevent marauders coming in, or convicts from escaping justice. The story implies there was only

---

[110] Judges 16:3

one gate from which anyone can enter or leave. We can imagine that the Philistines planned to close the gate as soon as they spotted Samson approaching it in the morning. This way, they could trap him inside the city. But that isn't what happened. Samson rose from his sleep in the middle of the night, went to the gate and uprooted it. He didn't just dismantle it; he carried it on his shoulders up a hill to throw it off a ridge so it could never be used to trap anyone again.

It is a foreshadowing of Christ's death and Resurrection, for when he breathed his last, death intended to swallow him up and keep him in the realm of the dead forever. But death was never the plan of God for humankind, to begin with; it is the result of original sin. Therefore, each human has to undergo death because of our weakened human nature. But how can Christ, the author of life – life itself – be kept prisoner by the gates of death? It is absurd! So Christ rose from his "sleep," broke down the gates of death to escape, and brought it to a place where it can never be used again. Sure, we have to die, but it is no longer an eternal death – we will resurrect with Christ at the end of time. That is his gift to us that we must be ever thankful for.

If the foreshadowing is not convincing, maybe the carrying of the wooden gates on Samson's shoulders to the top of a hill will convince you for it is the prefiguring of Christ carrying the cross to the ignominious hill that is Calvary.

Just like the rising smoke from the sacrifices in the Jerusalem temple, Christ's ascension into heaven shows that the Father accepts his sacrifice. By giving up himself, Jesus liberated us. No longer is mankind a slave to error. Although we still have to suffer a bodily death, the good news – no, the best news – is that death no longer has our soul in her shackles. It no longer is doomed to be separated forever from God who is life itself. Instead, grace is restored so our body and soul can together live with God for all eternity. Christ, then, is the fulfillment of Isaiah's vision, so we call Jesus *our liberator, our redeemer, our savior.*

Christ undid the disobedience of Adam while Mary undoes Eve's. Eve let the trust of God die in her heart, while Mary made the trust live again. Saint Irenaeus expressed this most eloquently: "The knot of Eve's disobedience was loosed by the obedience of Mary.

For what the virgin Eve had bound fast through unbelief, this did the virgin Mary set free through faith."[111] This is why Mary is also known as the *Undoer of Knots*.

Mary, however, is not the primary architect of this endeavor. Instead, God willed that she participate in his plan of redemption. By inviting Mary to be the mother of the Messiah, she was given a chance to "plead for mankind and save it from eternal ruin."[112] In this perspective, we can see Mary as a co-redeemer with her son, Jesus. We should not perceive it as a mother taking away glory from her son. Instead, we should see it as a good mother taking an interest in her son's activities – the salvation of souls.

When invoking this title, consider that: Mary gave birth to Jesus who saved us from spiritual death, and bought back the graces to combat our attraction to sin.

---

[111] Iranaeus, *Against Heresies*, 3, 22

[112] Lovasik, Lawrence. *Our Lady in Catholic Life*

VIRGIN MOST PRUDENT

PRUDENCE IS A CARDINAL VIRTUE that gets its name from *prudentia*, a contraction of *providentia*, which means, *to see ahead*. It means to be able to see what one's actions will result in. As a virtue, we employ prudence to discern what is good for us in union with God's will and choose the right means of achieving it.[113] Therefore, a prudent person uses practical reasoning and accurate information to decide on an action that will lead to material and spiritual good.

An example of this is in Christ's parable of the ten virgins who were waiting for the bridegroom to arrive.[114] Five were foolish, and five were prudent. The foolish ones didn't think to bring extra oil for their lamps, had to leave to buy some, and while they were away, the bridegroom came so that they missed the wedding feast. Those who were wise enough to prepare partook of the joyful festivities.

Part of prudence is considering a decision. Mary showed her prudence in considering the message of Gabriel during the Annunciation.[115] The Gospel of Luke says she "pondered what sort of greeting this might be."[116] In Scripture (the Old Testament at her time,) when God asked people to do something for him, they were always given strength using the words, "The Lord is with you." Joshua, Gideon, and David are examples of these. Accepting God's invitation disrupted and change their lives. So Mary pondered what sort of thing God might be asking of her and how it might alter her life.[117]

---

[113] CCC § 1806
[114] Matthew 25:2-13
[115] Luke 1:26-38
[116] Luke 1:29
[117] Sri, Edward. *The New Rosary in Scripture*. Servant Books. 2003

Prudence is also considering information to make the right decision. When the Angel Gabriel told her she would bear a child, Mary could have given her consent right away; but because the message came from God, Mary thought she ought to hear everything first.[118] She even asked, "How can this be" not through a lack of faith, but because she wanted to understand more. Prudence led her to make the right decision, and so she accepted to be the mother of the Messiah.

Prudence also allows us to reflect on things we might not understand at first. God didn't give Mary a set of instructions to follow. Instead, she tried to understand God's plan as it unfolded. So although she might not have fully understood events at the moment, she reflected on them.

One instance of this is when the shepherds visited the Holy Family in Bethlehem. They told her of the angels and the wonderful message to them. Joseph and Mary were "amazed" as it wasn't something they expected and probably didn't know what to make of it at that time. However, the Gospel says, "...Mary kept all these things, reflecting on them in her heart."[119]

Another instance of this is the losing and finding of Jesus in the temple.[120] When Mary asked Jesus, "Son, why have you done this to us? Your father and I have been looking for you with great anxiety." Jesus answered, "Did you not know that I must be in my Father's house?" Luke tells us Joseph and Mary's reaction: "But they did not understand what he said to them." Despite this, "his mother kept all these things in her heart." She would not have done so if she had no interest in eventually understanding it.

The Infancy Narratives of Luke, from where these two stories come from, were one of the last to be told and written.[121] After believing in a risen Christ, early Christians would have wanted to learn his origin story – just as they were accustomed to knowing about the hero in every Greek epic. Luke subtly implies that Mary is the source of these stories because "she pondered on them." Her

---

[118] Sheed, Frank J. *To Know Christ Jesus*
[119] Luke 2:19
[120] Luke 2:41-52
[121] Ralph, Margaret Nutting. *And God Said What?* Paulist Press. 2003

clear mind, unfettered from the effects of original sin, would have an increasing maturity in understanding them, thus allowing us to benefit by understanding her son even more.

Prudence also relies on the counsel of others. An instance of this was the time Joseph was warned in a dream to flee Herod's murderous rage and escape to Egypt.[122] Unlike Mary, Joseph never had direct messages from an angel. Instead, they always came to him in a dream. Joseph must have been a discerning person if he could determine if his dreams came from just his brain, or if it was of divine origin. Mary's prudence allowed her to agree with her husband's assessment without dissent. Her prudence saved her son from Herod's massacre of innocent children.[123]

Prudence is also determining actions to correctly put God ahead of ourselves. Mary was already betrothed to Joseph when the Angel Gabriel asked for her consent to bear a child; and this made them as good as married.[124] Because the child of Mary did not belong to Joseph, the public can plausibly misconstrue this as an act of adultery. Despite the possible penalty of death on herself (see *Holy Mary*), her prudence told her that accepting God's invitation was the right thing to do.

Prudence also kept her from abandoning her son during his Passion. There had been many false "messiahs" that appeared before Jesus, and they, their families, and all their followers were put to death. The concept of the Messiah was that of a warrior who would free Israel from foreign rule. So these "messiahs" were considered subversives who incited rebellion. The punishment for a capital offense such as this is crucifixion. Romans kept their subjects in line by crucifying subversives along pathways, thus embedding the images of the anguished victims in the minds of passersby. The disciples of Jesus would have certainly seen this sort of thing.

With this in context, it was a likely reaction for the apostles to flee and desert Christ the moment guards arrested him in the

---

[122] Matthew 2:13-15
[123] Matthew 2:16-18
[124] Sheed, Frank J. *To Know Christ Jesus*

Garden of Gethsemane. They hid from authorities afraid of being branded as rebels who ended being nailed to a cross.

Unlike them, John tells us that Mary planted herself beneath the cross as Christ drew breath after dying breath. She stood by Christ and attached herself to him. We can imagine she was so close to him that drop after drop of his precious blood drenched her while she stood under the cross. Prudence kept the fear, of suffering the same fate as her son, from not uniting herself with him all the way. Prudence told her that it was the right thing to do: she put her son ahead of her own life.

When invoking this title, consider that: Mary contemplates to do only the right things in the eyes of God.

Virgin Most Venerable

We honor Mary because of the role she played in the plan of salvation that makes her more venerable than any other human. During the Annunciation, Mary found out her older cousin Elizabeth was pregnant. After being told she would be the mother of the Messiah, she didn't bask in this great honor but instead, "left in haste for Judea" to assist Elizabeth. Upon seeing Mary, Elizabeth said, "Blessed are you among women..." Mary would have remembered that there were only two other women in the Septuagint version of the Old Testament that were called blessed. These are Jael, and Judith – and Elizabeth was comparing her to them through these words.[125]

The Book of Judges narrates the story of Jael. When Israel was growing up as a nation, they asked God for leaders to lead them. Instead of giving them a king, like the kingdoms around Israel, God gave them Judges. These were not arbiters of legal disputes. Instead, they were leaders God raised to "save them from the power of their plunderers."[126]

One such plunderer of God's chosen people was the army of King Jabin, led by the General, Sisera. A Judge by the name of Deborah was given the divine insight that the enemy army would be defeated, but the honor of killing Sisera would be given to a woman. Eventually, Barak, the leader of the Israelite army, did win the battle as God foretold. This forced Sisera to escape to a settlement in Zaanaim. There, a woman by the name of Jael welcomed him into her tent where she attended to him with milk and good food. After having his fill, he became drowsy and fell into a deep sleep. Jael took

---

[125] The Septuagint is the version the Church uses because it is what Christ and the New Testament writers used. We know this because they quoted from it.
[126] Judges 2:16

one of the tent pegs, stealthy crept to the sleeping Sisera, and with a mallet drove the tent peg through the temple of his head with so much force that it penetrated the ground beneath. Deborah's song extols Jael above women when they sing: "Most blessed of women be Jael." [127]

The Book of Judith tells her story. In the tale, Israelites in the town of Bethulia were suffering great anxiety because war was upon them. King Nebuchadnezzar of the Assyrians sent his top general, Holofernes, to subjugate lands that refused to serve him. When they cut off the water supply of the town, the Israelites became helpless prisoners in their own territory. Trapped in this siege, they thought of surrendering even if it meant they were to become slaves. Judith was the turning point. She had devised a plan and said, "I will perform a deed that will go down from generation to generation..."[128] If it sounds like the Magnificat,[129] that's because it foreshadows the Magnificat.

Implementing her plan, she pretended to flee from the doomed village to give information to Holofernes as a defector. The soldiers, including Holofernes, was captivated by her beauty and welcomed her into their camp. In a short time, she became their guest and earned their trust. One night, after the Assyrians pursued a night of heavy feasting, she was left alone with the general in his tent. He fell asleep after having taken too much wine. She then took his sword and with two blows beheaded Holofernes. With the Assyrian army without a leader, the Israelites easily drove them back. After that, no other army struck terror on the village again. Achior, a convert from the Assyrians, praised Judith with the words, "Blessed are you in every tent of Judah!"[130]

Just as Jael and Judith, Mary is called "blessed" because she is the realization of the prophecy of the "woman" who will crush the head of the enemy in Genesis when God promised the serpent, "I will put enmity between you and the woman, and between your

---

[127] Judges 5:23-27
[128] Judith 8:32
[129] Luke 1:46-55
[130] Judith 14:7

offspring and hers; They will strike at your head."[131] Because she is the fulfillment of this, we see statues and paintings of Mary with the head of a serpent crushed under her heel.

While the people of Bethulia were prisoners in their land, humankind was a prisoner of sin and death. To release us from this captivity, Christ became "sin" itself[132] and experienced death, which is the consequence of sin. It is there; in the devil's domain, that Christ defeated him and his works. Like Judith, then, Mary's birth to Jesus is like the unsheathing of a sword, Christ, who cuts off the head of the enemy in his own camp. Isn't it fascinating that Christ is the Word of God,[133] and the Word of God "is a two-edged sword penetrating even between soul and spirit, joints and marrow..."[134]

The typology is not yet done. Whereas John tells us, "And the Word became flesh and made his dwelling among us..."[135] the literal translation is, "he pitched his tent among us."[136] So by giving birth to Jesus, Mary is like Jael and Judith because the enemy's head was crushed in a "tent."

When invoking this title, consider that: Mary is *blessed among women* because she crushed the head of the enemy.

---

[131] Genesis 3:15
[132] Cf. 2 Corinthians 5:21
[133] John 1:1
[134] Hebrews 4:12
[135] John 1:14
[136] NABRE. Footnotes on John 1:14

Virgin Most Renowned

To be renowned means to be the most well known. When Mary visited Elizabeth, her *Magnificat* expresses what she has come to realize, "Behold, from now on will all ages call me blessed. The Mighty One has done great things for me, and holy is his name."[137] Coming from the lips of a girl in her early teens, her claim would have been absurd if it did not come true. But true to these prophetic words, every Catholic today calls her "blessed" in the *Hail Mary*.

We acknowledge her blessedness when we say she is the "preeminent and wholly unique member of the Church."[138] It is a declaration that she surpasses all of creation and we can't stop talking about it! She is like the rock star of all of God's creatures. While she is part of the Church, she holds a special place in it because she has an exclusive relationship with God that we don't have. Mary "is endowed with the high office and dignity of the Mother of the Son of God, and therefore she is also the beloved daughter of the Father and the temple of the Holy Spirit."[139]

No one else is the Mother of God. By giving birth to Jesus, we rightly give her that name. Although we are truly sons and daughters of God by adoption, Mary is a daughter of the Father in a unique way: She has been granted an utterly special likeness between her motherhood and the divine fatherhood.[140]

Adam and Eve were the son and daughter of God for he made them in his likeness. Sin, however, disfigured them. As an

---

[137] Luke 1:48
[138] CCC § 967, Lumen Gentium (#53) 1964, Marialis Cultus 1974, Rosarium Virginis Mariae 2002,
[139] *Lumen Gentium* #53
[140] St. Pope John Paul II, Mary's Relationship with the Trinity, L'Osservatore Romano, 17 January 1996, p. 11

inheritance, it continues to disfigure us almost to the point where God can hardly recognize us as his children. Baptism, however, reconfigures us to Christ so that we are "recognized" by God who allows us to become his true children through adoption. Mary, if we are to think of it, became a child of God in a different way. Since she was conceived without the stain of original sin, she was a child of God almost in the same sense that Eve was a child of God before the fall: her flesh was from mankind, and her spirit was untouched by sin or the stain of sin. From the moment of her creation, nothing separated Mary from being a child of God, and remained that way all her life. No other human can say that about himself or herself.

Part of her preeminence comes from being the spouse of the Holy Spirit. While we are all temples of the Holy Spirit, Mary is a literal and living temple when her womb became the dwelling place of God the Son. To the Holy Spirit, she is also, "his faithful spouse at the Annunciation, welcoming the Word of the true God..."[141]

She is also preeminent because she is Immaculate. It is a singular gift of spiritual perfection bestowed upon her that isn't given to any of God's other creatures. We reserve for her a *hyper-dulia* – a special reverence that we don't assign to the other saints.[142]

Even after the death of Christ, we understand that she held a special place with the apostles when she prayed with them, and they mention her by name.[143] This tradition was handed down to us today, making her the most well known and most recognized of God's creatures. No other saint receives as much public veneration as the Blessed Virgin.[144] Even in the liturgy, the Church has some memorial in her honor every month.

How wonderful it is that humanity has Mary to show God what perfection can be like for us. How marvelous there is a creature that meets God's absolute standards enough to be his mother. How breathtaking it is that we can be proud of someone who can reflect

---

[141] Redemtoris Mater #26

[142] CCC § 971, and cf. Chollet, col. 2407, and Bouquillon, Tractatus de virtute religionis, I, Bruges, 1880, 22 sq. Thesaurus ecclesiasticus, 1728. Encylcopedia of Catholicism 1995

[143] Cf. Acts 1:14

[144] Lovasik, Lawrence. *Our Lady in Catholic Life.*

the true image of the human race. Oh, Mary, all the earth acknowledges your worth.

When invoking this title, consider that: Mary's is the most well-known member of the Church.

Virgin Most Powerful

TWO MEANINGS OF POWER CAN APPLY TO MARY, and in both ways, we see her role as a "new Eve." In Genesis, as a result of Eve eating the forbidden fruit, God explained that there will be enmity between her and the serpent.[145] They will be enemies! Since Eve represents the human race and the serpent represents the devil, it means we have been in combat with the devil and evil since the fall of humankind.

The first meaning of *power* used for Mary is invincibility on the battlefield. An invincible warrior cannot be defeated and instead, does the defeating. So with this title, we recognize Mary as being victorious over all spiritual enemies and all evil.

In chapter 12 of the Book of Revelation, we read that Mary is the *woman* clothed with the sun and the moon at her feet. There, she meets her ancient enemy again, the serpent, but this time in a seemingly more formidable form as a dragon with seven heads. His tricks aren't new; he vomits a flood of lies as he did in the Garden of Eve. But the woman is victorious despite the malicious determination of her colossal adversary.

It might be difficult to envision Mary as a warrior, because warriors have battle scars, wear chainmail, defend themselves with heavy shields, brandish sharp swords that inflict damage, and keep war trophies. If it is impossible to imagine Mary this way, it is because she is not this kind of warrior. Her means of doing battle is not by launching offensive strategies, but rather quite the opposite. Her manner of doing battle with the enemy is through her quiet and humble obedience to God. When Mary accepted God's invitation to be the mother of the Son, she brought forth the Messiah that would

---

[145] Genesis 3:15

defeat the devil and all his works. Without the salvific actions of Jesus, humankind did not possess the graces needed to fight against the inclination to sin. Therefore, we can say that through Mary's obedience, the instrument to defeat evil, sin, error, and death was born in the person of Jesus. In a sense, the devil had some sort of free reign over mankind until Mary "unleashed" Christ, the weapon she kept in her womb. In this sense, she is a new Eve who is the mother of all the redeemed.

In her title *Tower of David*, we will revisit this power as she keeps as trophies the shields of her defeated opponents. (See *Tower of David*)

Mary is also known as "destroyer of heresies." This is another way she manifests her power against the devil – the "father of lies." Against the Nestorian Heresy, in 431 the Council of Ephesus dogmatically conferred the title *Mother of God* to Mary to protect the doctrine that Jesus is only one person with two distinct natures. When the Albigensian heresy wrongly taught Jesus could not be truly human because matter is evil, Mary gave the Rosary to St. Dominic in 1214 to battle this heresy. Later on, the Pelagian heresy spread the false teaching that the stain of original sin was not passed down to us. In effect, it meant we were already justified and so didn't need a savior. This wrongly reduced Christ's mission to being merely a teacher. In 1854, when Pope Pius IX defined the Immaculate Conception of Mary, it safeguarded the doctrine of original sin that was undone by the salvific actions of Christ.[146] In Lourdes, on 8 March 1958, Mary herself reinforced this truth when she declared to St. Bernadette, "I am the Immaculate Conception."

The other meaning of *power* we can apply to Mary is the gift in influencing others to do things. With Mary, we specifically mean her influence with God. Not that she can influence God – because nothing can alter God for he is unchanging – but that Mary will obtain anything for us that is in God's will.

She showed this at the Wedding at Cana. In this episode, Mary did not propose a solution; she just told her son the problem. The theologian Frank J. Sheed explains that Mary was not one who had

---

[146] *Munificentissimus Deus*

bright ideas to dismiss what God wants. He suggests that Mary must have been prompted by the Holy Spirit to ask for this miracle. By doing this, Sheed is alluding that Mary was being her obedient self. This, he says, completes the identity of the "New Eve." Whereas Eve, a virgin, agreed to do what a bad angel told her to do (the devil in Eden) and prompted Adam to commit his first shameful act; Mary, also a virgin, agreed to what a good angel told her to do (Gabriel in the Annunciation) and suggested that the new Adam do his first glorious act.[147]

Here we realize that Mary will indeed obtain for us what we need. However, since she is entirely in communion with God and his will, she will not gain things for us that are contrary to what he wants for us. She is powerful, yes, but always within God's loving will that knows what is good for us.

This should remind us of the Miraculous Draught of Fish.[148] Saint Peter came back from a bad night of fishing without a catch. When Jesus told him to go back and cast the nets, he begrudgingly did so. Did not Peter have the right to be reluctant? Peter was a seasoned fisherman who knew ebb and flow of the tides. He knew where and when fish were in the sea; how would a carpenter know more about fishing than a fisherman would? But, the Gospel of Luke tells us, the resulting haul was so massive that the nets were breaking. They were amazed and afraid because they couldn't understand what had just happened.

Seemingly unrelated, Jesus then told them, "from now on you will catch men." But Christ meant it to be a lesson for them: even if it doesn't seem reasonable when Christ tells them to fish, they will fish with power. So when Christ tells them to catch men, they will catch men with power. When Our Lady, in Cana, admonishes us to "do what he tells you," we do it because when Christ tells us to do things, we will do it with power.

This should give us an insight, too, to the secret of why Mary is most powerful: it is because of her humble obedience to do what God asks her to do.

---

[147] Sheed, Frank J. *To Know Christ Jesus.*
[148] Luke 5:1-11

When invoking this title, consider that: Mary defeats all the enemies of God's people simply by doing his will.

VIRGIN MOST MERCIFUL

IN CHRISTIANITY, the word *merciful* is mostly associated with the forgiveness of sins. For example, we rely on God's mercy that we do not deserve or merit.

God gave free will to all his intelligent creatures. Since he transcends time, he has seen all our actions in the past, present, and future. God saw the fall of mankind and the intervention of a savior. In his mercy, he put together such a plan. Included in that plan was a woman who would give birth to the Second Person of the Blessed Trinity. This woman, Mary, was prevented from inheriting the effects of original sin. Because of this, she was conceived without any sin for God to forgive. It is what we call a *prevenient grace* – a term to describe a gift God gave to her even before she existed. Since it pre-existed her, she could not have possibly done anything to merit it. In the words of St. Pope John Paul II, Mary "experienced mercy in an exceptional way."[149] Because of this, Mary is the created masterpiece of God's mercy. As the fruit of this Divine Mercy, it would not be farfetched to think that she also possessed it in a human capacity.

Mary is also the bride of the Holy Spirit in the sense that it was the Holy Spirit who overshadowed her to conceive Jesus. The Holy Spirit is the living love between the Father and the Son. Since the flower of love is mercy, the love of the Holy Spirit must have flowered within her – both literally as Christ, and figuratively as a result of being "touched" by the Holy Spirit. She must possess some of this mercy, for how can a fruit not possess some of the sweetness of the tree that nurtured it with its sugary sap?

---

[149] St. Pope John Paul II. *Dives in Misericordia*, Section 9

While *clemens*, the original Latin word used in the Litany, does mean *merciful*, it can also mean *compassionate*, *mild*, and *lenient*.

We ask Mary to bring our supplications to Christ when we need rescue from danger, cure of disease, and means to material needs. We do this because we know she is compassionate to us.

In the Wedding at Cana,[150] Mary perceptively understood the predicament the lack of wine could result in and told Jesus about the situation. If she manifested her compassion to the bride and groom even without their knowing, what more can she do for us who implore her assistance, now that she is in heaven and has a clear understanding of our misery.[151]

Mary is mild in the sense that she repays evil with kindness. When St. Paul describes Jesus as someone sinless who was made into sin,[152] we imagine all the terrible and evil things humankind can inflict on a person. It is as if sin itself – that lack of love for God and neighbor – was heaped on Christ. He became the perfect example of a person who the world has turned against. Mary must have been heartbroken to see her son in such a pitiful state. But despite the horrible things we humans have done to her son, she still accepted to be our mother when Christ gave her to us from the cross.[153]

We can also see Mary as being lenient in the sense that she "stays the hand of Divine Justice."[154] Indirectly, she is the antidote to the poison that Eve brought into humanity that brings us spiritual death. For through her consent to be the mother of Christ, she became an instrument to bring Jesus – whose name means *Yahweh Saves* – into the world. Whereas humankind deserved eternal separation from God, Mary's *fiat* allowed God's plan, to mend the broken relationship between God and man, become a reality.

If that were not enough, we believe she intercedes for us tirelessly in the effort to lead all sinners back to God so that we may not receive the justice that we so rightly deserve.

---

[150] John 2:1-12
[151] Lovasik, Lawrence. *Our Lady in Catholic Life*. p.281
[152] 2 Corinthians 5:21
[153] John 19:26
[154] Lovasik, Fr. Lawrence. *Our Lady in Catholic Life*. p.281

Saint Bridgette of Sweden had a mystical experience when Jesus allowed her to "eavesdrop" on his conversation with his mother. "My mother, ask of me whatever you wish," Jesus said. Saint Bridgette heard Mary's request, "I ask mercy for sinners." Indeed, our mother continues to keep us from getting the penance we deserve.

So with St. Bernard of Clairvaux, we say to Mary, "We praise your virginity, and we admire your humility. But your mercy has an even sweeter taste for us sinners. We have a greater love for your mercy; we remember it and call upon it more often. Who then could measure, Blessed Lady, the length and breadth, the height and depth of your mercy? Its length truly stretches out to the last day, so that you may come to the assistance of all who call upon it. Its breadth spans the whole universe, so that the whole earth is full of your mercy. Its height is so great that it brought about the restoration of the heavenly city. Its depth accomplished the redemption of those who sat in darkness and in the shadow of death."

When invoking this title, consider that: Mary continually pleads for our forgiveness.

Virgin Most Faithful

A PERSON IS CONSIDERED FAITHFUL when she or he keeps promises that were made. A person is also regarded as faithful in a religious sense when she or he fulfills obligations to God. In both these cases, Mary can be said to be faithful.

When the Angel Gabriel announced to Mary that she was to be the mother of the Messiah, she was perplexed as to how that would happen, considering she made a vow of perpetual virginity. We can see why it was mystifying because it was a vow to God and it seemed to her that God was asking her to break that vow so she can be a mother. It was only through the explanation of the Angel Gabriel that she understood this would happen without losing her virginity. When she was shown the way, she consented. But her *fiat* was the start of another vow to be the mother of the Messiah. To be a mother does not only mean giving birth, but to nurture, raise, and keep one's child from harm.

In Jewish tradition, every woman who gives birth to a male child was considered "impure" and must keep away from the temple or anything sacred for forty-one days. That is eight days from birth to circumcision and another thirty-three days after. The mother's blood is to be purified, and a purification sacrifice is to be presented: a lamb for a burnt offering and a young pigeon or turtledove for a sin offering. Those who could not afford a lamb could instead offer two turtledoves or two young pigeons. We see Mary being faithful to the law when she fulfilled this requirement.

We believe Mary was immaculately conceived and that she was aided by the Holy Spirit to remain sinless the rest of her life. So if this is true, she did not need to purify herself because she was pure and sinless. Nevertheless, because she is faithful, she obeyed this law that God gave through Moses.

Another requirement of parents of any firstborn is to "buy" him back from God. Because God spared the firstborn of Israel during the original Passover, all of them belong to God. So as a law,[155] all parents must redeem their firstborn from God for five shekels. It is ironic that Joseph and Mary should redeem Jesus from God because he is God who is the Redeemer himself. But they did so anyway because they were faithful to the law.

What Mary did in the temple is even more than what was required: she offered Jesus to God. In Deuteronomy, the tribe of Levi was chosen to "stand before the Lord" to serve him. This was because they were the only tribe who did not join in the worship of the golden calf. When the Gospel of Luke uses the Greek word, "paristanai" to describe how Mary presents Jesus to God, it is a reference to the Levites that remind us of sacrifice and priesthood. It suggests Mary was handing over Jesus entirely to God in his service as a priest who would sacrifice a victim, but in the case of Christ, he would be the priest and victim.

The scene is also reminiscent of Hannah handing over Samuel to Levi[156] where Samuel is destined to be a prophet just as Jesus would be.

When Simeon told Mary that "a sword will pierce through your own soul," it did not deter her from keeping her promise to raise and nurture her child. When St. Joseph was warned in a dream that Herod is searching for the child to destroy him, Mary must have feared for her son's life knowing that the evil king murdered his father-in-law, his mother-in-law, his first wife, and two of his own sons. Joseph "rose and took the child and his mother by night and departed for Egypt."[157] Mary, as a faithful wife, went without question even if a night journey would be uncomfortable, and fraught with danger from bandits or wild animals. We recognize here Mary's faithfulness to her vow to God, as well as her marriage vows to Joseph to go where the father of the family goes.

The Gospel of Matthew tells us they returned from Egypt and settled in Nazareth; and there, the Gospel of Luke tells us, Jesus

---

[155] Exodus 13:2, 12-13
[156] 1 Samuel 1
[157] Matthew 2:14

grew up.[158] It is at this time Mary continued to nurture and raise Jesus, fulfilling her vow to be the mother of the Messiah.

All that time Jesus belonged to her alone. But in Cana, at her suggestion to do his first miracle, Jesus would become a public figure. She must have realized that he would no longer be hers alone, but would have to share him with the entire world. We have to consider that it must be painful for a mother to let go of her son, and despite this, Mary is faithful in making available to us the Messiah of God.

Finally, in the hour of Christ's deepest humiliation: naked and crucified, rejected by the Jews and priests, and abandoned by almost all of his closest disciples, Mary can still be found under the cross. For any human, it is but natural to cry out to our mother when we are in pain. But Christ did not need to do that for he saw his Mother there already participating in his suffering with him. She demonstrated her compassion – literally from "com" and "passion," which means, "to be one with Christ's Passion." Even if the family and friends of crucified insurgents were usually killed, Mary was undeterred by this danger to remain faithful as a mother and be with her son until the conclusion of his earthly mission.

So when Jesus gave her to us to be the mother of the church,[159] we can be assured she will be faithful to her motherly responsibilities to us as a Church and as individuals.

At baptism, we made three promises: to renounce Satan, and all his works, and all his empty promises. Because Mary is our mother, we can be assured she will come to our aid in being faithful to these vows.

When invoking this title, consider that: Mary is faithful to her vows to God, to the Law, and to her motherhood to us.

---

[158] Matthew 2:23, Luke 2:40
[159] John 19:26

MIRROR OF JUSTICE

IN SCRIPTURE, the word *just* is synonymous with *upright, righteous,* and *without blame*. It is used to describe people who lived virtuous lives. The Book of Genesis describes Noah as a *"just man."*[160] The letter of James asks, "Was not Abraham our father *justified* by works..."[161] The letter of Peter, likewise, portrays Lot as *just* and *righteous*.[162] The list goes on with Job, King David, Simeon, and Joseph the husband of Mary.[163]

The standards of *being just* – also known as *justice* – are the moral principles set by God through his commandments. Thus, *justice* is the obedience to God's laws. The author of Kings says it quite poetically: "you have not seen my servant David, who *kept my commandments*, and who followed me with all his heart, to do that only which was *right* in my eyes..."[164]

God is all-good, so he is the standard of morality. This would mean all the just, and righteous men and women partially reflect God's virtue. It is only partial because tiny flaws in the character and nature of these men and women distort the image of God in them. But when we say Mary is the *Mirror of Justice*, it means she is a mirror without any flaw that can perfectly reflect God's holiness.

If humankind were made in God's image, and Mary is immaculate – meaning without flaw or blemish – then God's virtues are reflected by her soul as in a perfect mirror.[165] Therefore, she reflects the humility, chastity, meekness, patience, mercy, faith,

---

[160] Genesis 6:9
[161] James 2:21
[162] 2 Peter:7-8 (Italics are mine for emphasis)
[163] Job 1:8, 1 King 14:8, Luke 2:25, Matthew 1:19
[164] 1 Kings 14:8 (Italics are mine for emphasis.)
[165] Lovasik, Lawrence. *Our Lady in Catholic Life*. p288

hope, and charity God has in the person of her son Jesus. Since Jeremiah called Christ, "The Lord our justice,"[166] Mary, who flawlessly reflects Christ, can be called the *Mirror of Justice*.

A mirror is also something we look at to check ourselves. We adjust our clothes or make-up if there is something wrong with what we see in the mirror. So when we look at Mary, the *Mirror of Justice*, we check ourselves against what we see in her and make corrections in our spiritual life. Thus, she is our model of virtue we use as the standard to improve ourselves accordingly in our efforts to be a disciple of Christ.

When invoking this title, consider that: Mary perfectly reflects God's goodness.

---

[166] Jermiah 23:6

Seat of Wisdom

THE ORIGINS OF THIS TITLE CAN BE LINKED TO TEMPLE WORSHIP of the Jews during the time of Christ. The Hebrews were so in awe at wisdom that they wrote about it in what we call the "Wisdom Books" in the Bible: Job, Psalms, Proverbs, Ecclesiastes, Song of Songs, Widsom, and Sirach. We learn from these books that the definition of *wisdom* is a "Fear of the Lord." It is the humbling of oneself in obedience and reverence to God

In the Book of Proverbs, wisdom is personified as a woman called, "Lady Wisdom." Therefore, it shouldn't be at all surprising to find out that six hundred years before Christ, they honored *Lady Wisdom* in the temple under a different but interesting name: *Mother of the Lord.*[167] This was not a reference to Mary, but a way of poetically expressing God being so wise as if it was (Lady) wisdom that gave birth to him. Because early Christians still considered themselves as Jews, it wasn't difficult for them to see Mary the *Mother of the Lord*, to be "Lady Wisdom."

The previous title *Mirror of Justice* reminds us of a passage in the Book of Wisdom that defines wisdom as, "the reflection of eternal light, the spotless mirror of the power of God, the image of his goodness."[168] So if Mary is a perfect reflection of God (see Mirror of Justice), and wisdom is defined as a "spotless mirror of God," then Mary is *wisdom* itself in a figurative sense too. It isn't some connection we are desperately trying to make, but a reiteration of what Jesus said about his mother. When a woman in a crowd told him, "Blessed is the womb that carried you and the breasts at which you nursed," he replied, "Rather, blessed are those who hear the

---

[167] Baker, Margaret. *The Images of Mary in the Litany of Loreto*, Usus Antiquior. July 2010.p112
[168] Book of Wisdom 7:26

word of God and observe it."[169] Christ corrected the woman saying Mary is blessed not because she is his mother, but because Mary obeys God's laws. In the biblical definition of *wisdom*, Mary is *wise*, in this way.

In this sense, we see Mary as the *Seat of Wisdom* as one who possessed and practiced wisdom in the highest degree.[170] But in another sense, the title can refer to her as a real seat where wisdom – her son, Jesus – sat.

As St. Augustine explained the Blessed Trinity, the Father thinks of himself, and this thought is the Son. Since the Father is all knowing, the idea of himself is perfect: whatever the Father is, his thought also is. Putting this together with what St. Thomas Aquinas said, "God is the sheer act of being itself" we can understand that if the Father is existence itself, then so must the perfect thought of himself be existence itself; thus another distinct living person. This thought of the Father is what St. John refers to as *The Word*.[171] Because the Father is a pure spirit with no mouth, *The Word*, is a figure of speech to describe his thought.

Since God is all wise, his thought – his *Word* – is wisdom itself, and this time no longer allegorical but literal as another person in Jesus. Therefore, Jesus is Wisdom.

Another way *The Word* is Wisdom is he is all knowing: he knows everything about everything in all of eternity. God transcends time; thus, all history is present to him. So even before he flung the universe into existence, he already knew mankind would be tempted and would fall. God knew he would have to suffer as a human in the person of Jesus. In addition, we might say in our human terms that the Father "suffered" too at seeing his only begotten son suffer. Regardless of this, God chose to create us knowing full well it will cost him some suffering. Such is the love of God who gives without counting the cost. So at the point in history when the Son obeys the Father's will to become human, suffer, and die for the salvation of mankind, the Son empties himself out of love. As if his life wasn't enough, even after his death, blood and

---

[169] Luke 11:27-28
[170] Lovasik, Fr. Lawrence. *Our Lady in Catholic Life*. p 290
[171] John 1:1

water poured out of his dead body when a centurion pierced his side – utterly emptying him. Nothing is left of him. Thus, Christ reflects God's unconditional love through his obedience – which is the definition of *wisdom*.

So we give this title to Mary because when the Son of God assumed flesh in the womb of Mary, she literally became the Seat of Wisdom. When the infant Jesus sat on her lap, she became his throne and the Seat of Wisdom. Finally, when she embraced his bloodstained body after it was taken down from the cross, she became the Seat of Wisdom.

When invoking this title, consider that: Mary exhibits wisdom when she obeys God. Her body is the "throne" of her son.

CAUSE OF OUR JOY

MARY IS THE CAUSE OF OUR JOY because she gave birth to our Savior, Jesus Christ – who is our joy. In Scripture, a return as well as a communion with God causes joy.

When Babylon overran Jerusalem, they exiled learned men and natural leaders as a preemptive move to thwart any attempt of a retaliatory rebellion. Jeremiah tells us the exile is so sorrowful that "In Ramah is heard the sound of sobbing, bitter weeping! Rachel mourns for her children, she refuses to be consoled for her children – they are no more!"[172]

To put this in context, God changed the name of Jacob to *Israel*. It is from his twelve children where the twelve tribes of Israel are named. By the time of Jeremiah, both Jacob and Rachel (Jacob's wife) are long dead. Rachel is buried in Ramah, and since she is the matriarchal ancestor of the people Israel, we can understand why she is sorrowful when we realize how difficult it was for her to conceive children (See *Queen of Patriarchs*) whose descendants were only to be taken away into exile.

But Jeremiah prophesied a return of the exiles back into Jerusalem. The vision is poetic as he continues: "Shout with joy for Jacob... Look I will bring them back from the land of the north... Then young women shall make merry and dance, young men and old as well. I will turn their mourning into joy."[173]

Never was there such joy in Israel! Psalm 126 tells us: "When the Lord restored the captives of Zion we thought we were dreaming. Then our mouths were filled with laughter; our tongues sang for joy. [174]

---

[172] Jeremiah 31:15
[173] Jeremiah 31:7-14
[174] Psalm 6:1-6

The parables of Jesus also express a deep joy when the shepherd finds his lost sheep, when a woman finds her lost coin, and when the Father reunites with his lost Prodigal son.[175] All of the parables cause joy by the return of something or someone.

Joy is also the result when there is a communion with God. When the unborn John the Baptist meets the unborn Jesus, St. Elizabeth tells Mary that her son "leaped for joy."[176] When Jesus called Zaccheus, he welcomed Our Lord "joyfully."[177]

Salvation history is a return to God – a communion (from *com* "with," and *unus* "union"). Humankind was made to be with God. We can see this when he walked side-by-side with humankind in the Garden of Eden. When humankind rejected God, it is proof he loved us so much that he didn't force himself on us. Instead, like the prodigal son, we left God's "house." Genesis describes it very poetically as an exile from Eden.

Mary's *fiat* to God's plan was the turning point of this exile. For when she accepted to be the mother of the Messiah, the eternal God, who transcends space and time, became flesh in the confines of her womb. In that one stroke, the Protoevangelium in Genesis, where God promised the serpent that his head will be crushed by the woman and her child,[178] became a reality.

It is Christ's Passion and death that ransomed us, and it is his Ascension that ended our exile. The Father accepted his son, who is fully human, into heaven. So when we attach ourselves to the Church in Baptism, we follow Christ's path to heaven. It does make sense, doesn't it: because the Church is the mystical Body of Christ, and if we are part of it, we go with it to where it is – in heaven.

Because Jesus brings us back to our true home where we are united with God, he is our joy; and Mary is the "cause" of our joy.

Another way to interpret the title is that she causes joy in us. We are joyful because she is our mother. If we could choose our mother, we'd probably choose the best. God could do that, and from all eternity, God chose Mary to be his mother – a mother he gave to

---

[175] Luke 15:3-32
[176] Luke 1:44
[177] Luke 19:6
[178] Genesis 3:15

us when he told St. John who represented the church: "Behold thy mother."[179] Shouldn't it give us great joy to have the best mother God could create?

Her Assumption also gives us joy because we know that humans are capable of virtue and deserving of heaven. Through her example, we are filled with joyful hope that we, too, will one day return to our true home. It is a "double joy" because we both return to God where we will be united with him.

When invoking this title, consider that: Mary gave birth to the one would end our exile and bring us back into communion with God.

---

[179] John 19:27

Spiritual Vessel

W HEN IT WAS FINISHED, the temple was essential to the Jews because it became the permanent place for the Holy of Holies where the presence of God resided. But it wasn't always that way; the tabernacle used to be in a tent that traveled with the Israelites as they made their way from Egypt to the Promised Land.

As part of their worship, vessels were used as containers of sacred things or for rituals. The Ark of the Covenant contained manna, the Ten Commandments, and the rod of the high priest. Some vessels were used to collect blood from sacrificed animals to be spilled in the corners of the altar. Still, others were used to pour wine on the altar as a libation. Because they were not used for anything else, they are said to be *consecrated* – that is, set aside for a divine purpose.

While the temple was being built, it was King David who collected these sacred vessels to be brought to Jerusalem and used in the temple when it was finished.

Being a *Spiritual Vessel*, then, is a symbolic way of saying Mary was the container of the Holy Spirit because it was the Holy Spirit that overshadowed her and dwelt in her.

In a larger scale, Mary is like the temple for when Jesus was inside her womb; she was the container of the tangible presence of God. In the late Middle Ages, an illustrated book titled *Speculum Humanae Salvatoris* (Mirror of Human Salvation) was used to teach popular theology to the illiterate. It would compare images from the Old Testament as a *type* (or foreshadowing) to something or someone in the New Testament. In that book, the Temple of Solomon is shown to be a foreshadowing of Mary.[180]

---

[180] *Speculum Humanae Salvatoris*

More so, it isn't difficult to compare her to a sacred vessel because we believe in her perpetual virginity before, during, and after Christ's birth. (See *Holy Virgin of Virgins*) We can see in this that she and her womb are consecrated for a divine purpose – not to be used for anything else but the service of God. So just as a vessel whose value comes from keeping the treasure within, Mary is a reflection of the psalms: "All the glory of the king's daughter is within golden border..."[181]

Another way of looking at this title is to see how it describes Mary being spiritually minded.[182] She internalized what her senses took in and saw them with the eyes of faith. Sometimes she didn't fully understand things, but she "kept all these words, pondering them in her heart."[183] A reflection of these things is a meditation – a conversation with God – in a quest to understand them. It is a quest to understand what God wants of her. In this sense, as a *Spiritual Vessel*, Mary kept spiritual things in her.

When invoking this title, consider that: Mary's body is a home of the Holy Spirit, and her womb is the sacred vessel that contained God-made-man.

---

[181] Psalm 45:13 (or 14)
[182] Newman, Bl. John Henry. *Meditations and Devotions.*
[183] Luke 2:19 and 2:51

VESSEL OF HONOR

IT WAS GOD WHO COMMANDED MOSES to make vessels for liturgical use.[184] The use of vessels in liturgy continues today as it was done in temple worship by our "older cousins" the Jews. In the celebration of the Holy Eucharist today, for example, the host is placed on a paten; the wine, in a chalice. When the priest says the words of institution, "this is my body... this is my blood..." these two vessels are the most honored of all because they hold the body and blood of Our Lord, Jesus Christ. The General Instruction of the Roman Missal says, "Among the requisites of the celebration of the Mass, the sacred vessels are held in special honor, especially the chalice and paten..."[185]

In the beautiful mystery of the Incarnation, Mary became this vessel of honor *for she was to hold the flesh and blood of the incarnate Son of God.*[186] For nine months, she was a living chalice that contained our Lord. As a vessel, she becomes a reminder of Our Lord's humility to allow himself to be contained even if he cannot be contained, to be protected even if he is all powerful, and nourished even if he is self-sufficient.

In a letter of St. Paul to Timothy, he wrote, "Therefore, if anyone cleanses himself from these things, he will be a vessel for honor, sanctified, useful to the Master, prepared for every good work."[187] This section of the letter talks about making one acceptable to God by being blameless. If Mary was to be a vessel of honor so she can be useful for the Master, it was only fitting that she be spotless, even from the stain of original sin. So "Mary was,

---

[184] Exodus 27:3, 40:10
[185] GIRM 327
[186] Lovasik, Lawrence. *Our Lady in Catholic Life.* p299
[187] 2 Timothy 2:21

from the first moment of her conception, by a singular grace and privilege of almighty God and by the merits of Jesus Christ, Savior of the human race, preserved immune from all stain of original sin."[188]

One might get tempted to think that she was created immaculate just so that the stain of original sin would not be transmitted to her son Jesus. But that is to put conditions on Christ's incarnation as if our Redeemer needed someone to redeem him. Jesus, who is God, did not need to be cleansed of the stain of original sin because he could never have contracted it in the first place.[189] Therefore, the Immaculate Conception is not a requirement, but a grace! We should see it as a gift from God to honor his mother. This is another way we can see that Mary is a *Vessel of Honor.*

Her honor rings out throughout the ages when she sang Israel's song in the Magnificat, "all generations shall call me blessed."[190] With this title, we continue to proclaim her blessedness because God honored her in a way none of us are.

When invoking this title, consider that: We honor Mary because her womb contained the body and blood of Christ.

---

[188] CCC § 496, Pius IX, Ineffabilis Deus (1854)

[189] Erlenbush, Fr.Ryan *The New Theological Movement*, 12-8-2011. Web http://newtheologicalmovement.blogspot.com/2011/12/was-jesus-immaculately-conceived.html

[190] Luke 1:48

Singular Vessel of Devotion

DEVOTION COMES FROM THE LATIN DEVOVERE, which means a commitment to something related to God's service. The real test of devotion is not merely regular activity but doing things cheerfully and promptly despite their difficulty.

From the *Protoevangelium of James*, we learn that Mary wanted to devote herself to God's service in the temple. It meant being a virgin so she can dedicate her life without distraction. But from the onset, it wasn't to be easy. When the Angel Gabriel greeted her, "the Lord is with you," Luke tells us that she was troubled by the greeting.[191] (See *Mother Inviolate* and *Virgin Most Prudent*)

Then when Gabriel told her she will be with child, her "how can this be?" helps us understand that she did not intend to have sexual relations with Joseph even if they were betrothed or married. (See *Mother Most Chaste*) We also discussed that conceiving a child that isn't her husband's is equivalent to being stoned to death for adultery. (See *Holy Mary*) Despite all of these she chose to accept her role, and when she did her entire life became dedicated to her son.

From Scripture, we read that her life wasn't comfortable after she chose to be the mother of the Messiah, but she did it all for Jesus. She had to go to Bethlehem despite being ripe and could give birth at any moment. In Bethlehem, she had to suffer rejection when no place would take them in despite her condition. She had to give birth in an animal's feeding station inside a cave that was certainly not suitable for any mother to give birth. Later, we find out she couldn't afford to offer a lamb in the Presentation in the Temple. When she suggested for Jesus to perform his first miracle,

---

[191] Luke 2:28

it was to give him to us – knowing that there may no longer be alone time for just the both of them. During Christ's Passion, she quietly accepted God's plan of Salvation as she witnessed the cruelty heaped upon him. Maybe thinking her role was over, she nevertheless accepted her son's will for her to be our mother– thus extending her role in God's plan of salvation.

From this quick summary of her public life, we know of no hesitation or misery on Mary's part in the service of her son. She is a reflection of wisdom for, "Her conversation has no bitterness, nor her company any tediousness..."[192] She joyfully accepted all of this when she gave her herself to be the "slave" of the Lord. (See *Holy Mary*)

Indeed a "slave" was she by doing everything for Christ's sake. Thus, hers is a real and perfect devotion to her son, before, during, and after his life and death. Even today, her maternal nurturing continues long after her life on earth has ended. No other person is dedicated to her son in this way; thus, she is genuinely a *Singular Vessel of Devotion.*

God granted her request of being a virgin dedicated to the service in the temple in a magnificent way for she became the "temple" itself (See *Spiritual Vessel*). Like a vessel that contained the fragrant smell of salvation, she is like the alabaster jar that opened its contents in service of Christ,[193] whose perfume fills the entire Church with her sweet odor.

When invoking this title, consider that: Mary is genuinely committed to the service of God.

---

[192] Wisdom 8:16
[193] Matthew 26:7

Mystical Rose

THE CONNECTION OF SAINTS TO FLOWERS IS STRONG. There is a beautiful story of a Church in Mentosca d'Agesco in Austria, of a cut lily that devotees placed in the hand of the statue of Saint Anthony of Padua. What is remarkable is that it remained fragrant and alive for almost a year – only to produce a second bloom that filled the church with its aroma.

This association with flowers even manifests itself in religious art. Saint Dominic, for example, is usually portrayed in paintings with a lily as a symbol of purity. Saint Catherine of Siena has a lily for her emblem. Saint Agnes, and St. Sebastian are commonly depicted with a palm branch. Saint Barnabas is associated with an olive branch; and St. Ursicinus, a fleur-de-lis.

Saint Joseph is usually depicted with a lily blooming from his staff. This imagery came from a scene in the *Protoevangelium of James* when the High Priest was intent on finding a protector for Mary. Inspired by Isaiah 11:1: "and there shall come forth a rod out of the root of Jesse, and a flower shall rise up out of his root," he instructed all the single men of the House of David (who is the son of Jesse) to bring their wooden rods to the altar. When Joseph put his staff on the altar, it bloomed the same way Aaron's dead rod miraculously bloomed.[194] They serve as a reminder that, through God, it isn't impossible for a virgin to conceive and give birth.[195]

As instructed by an angel in a dream, Joseph named the son of Mary, "Jesus." This made Joseph his legal guardian, and this attached Jesus to Joseph's lineage. (See *Holy Mary*) This is important because Jesus becomes a "son of David" who is the one that truly

---

[194] Numbers 17:8
[195] *Biblia Pauperum*: Nativity

fulfills Isaiah's prophecy of a shoot blooming from Jesse's stump; Jesus becomes this king of the Davidic kingdom.

Saints also emit what is called an *odor of sanctity*. It is alternately used figuratively or literally. In the figurative sense, the odor of sanctity pertains to the "fragrance" of a soul that is in a state of grace. A "state of grace" means one is attached to God, thus sharing his divine life. A soul connected to God, therefore, is alive, whereas one that isn't is dead, and anything dead smells of rot.

In the literal sense, some saints actually emitted a pleasing scent. For example, the blood from Saint Pio's stigmata smelled of flowers. Saint Teresa of Avila and Saint Maravillas of Jesus emitted a strong flowery bouquet after their death. Saint Therese of Lisieux – also called the *Little Flower* – produced a strong fragrant aroma of roses after she died.

Saints, then, are like flowers because they emit a "fragrance" just as flowers do. In the Song of Songs, the husband tells her bride, "You are a private garden, my treasure, my bride..."[196] Since the Song of Songs is an allegorical canticle expressing God's love for his Church – which is his bride and mystical body – he regards it as a garden. If the Church were a garden, then saints would be "mystical flowers" in that garden.

In the Davidic Kingdom, there is what is called the *Gebirah* – the queen mother. Because kings after David were polygamous, it became difficult to determine who was queen. So it is said the Israelites emulated eastern kingdoms where it is the king's mother who they crowned queen. Therefore, because Jesus is a king in the line of David, it is through this tradition that his mother, Mary, is the queen. That is why she is Our Queen. That is why we call her "Our Lady."

In the botanical world, the rose is the queen of flowers. Therefore, if saints are mystical flowers, then Mary is the mystical rose whose spiritual beauty and fragrance outclasses them all.

Mary is like a white rose in her purity. She is like a red rose stained by the blood of Christ as she kept him company under the cross. Mary is also like a gold rose as she rejoices in the bliss and

---

[196] Song of Songs 4:12

glory of her son's Resurrection. The green leaves of the rose express hope – as she is the fulfillment of hope for which we aspire.[197]

There are miracles involving roses that are very much affiliated with Mary. On 29 December 1336, some mercenaries followed a pregnant Egidia Mathis as she walked on a street that leads to Turin in Italy. When she sensed their intention to harm her, she ran to a pillar that had an image of Our Lady, and prayed to her for help. As an apparition, Mary drove the men away. Nearby blackthorn bushes, which were covered in ice, suddenly bloomed with white flowers even if it was winter. Until today, the same shrubs bloom out of season year after year.[198] Botanists who study this phenomenon are baffled as to why it annually blooms out of season. Maybe they would have understood the miraculous occurrence if they realized the botanical name of the blackthorn is *Rosaceae* that belongs to the rose family.

In 1531, Mexico, Mary asked Juan Diego to gather flowers to convince the local bishop of her apparitions to the former. Juan Diego brought the flowers to her, and she arranged them on his cloak. When he opened the cloak before the foreigner, Archbishop Zumarraga, the flowers fell to the floor, and an image of Mary formed on the cloak. The image was not the only miracle for the flowers were Castilian roses that are not indigenous to Mexico. What is fascinating is that they were native to the bishop's homeland. The image of Mary on the cloak became known as *Our Lady of Guadalupe*.

While a rose is beautiful and royal, its thorns can also symbolize suffering. Like a rose growing among thorns, Mary, despite being queen, was not spared from trials and sorrows. (See *Singular Vessel of Devotion* and *Queen of Martyrs*) The height of her sorrows, any loving mother would know, is the suffering she endured with Christ during his Passion. Every blow, every lash, every act of cruelty heaped upon him was felt by his mother emotionally and psychologically. The Romans reserved crucifixion

---

[197] Lovasik, Lawerence. *Our Lady in Catholic Life*.p395
[198] Curiously, the only time they didn't bloom where 1941 and 1939, when each World War began.

for the worst convicts, so Christ's humiliation is hers too as she accompanied him on the way to Calvary where bystanders saw her as the mother of a repulsive criminal. The shame must have been so great she might as well be an outlaw herself – at least that must have been the feeling.

So Mary, as a mystical rose, reminds us that we aren't saved from suffering; instead, we are saved through it. She presents to us a model that in spite of being immersed in sorrow she can still be beautiful and emit that bouquet of holiness.

When invoking this title, consider that: Mary is the most beautiful and fragrant flower in God's "garden" of saints.

TOWER OF DAVID

THE ORIGIN OF THIS TITLE can come from two objects in Scripture: the Holy of Holies, and a strategic watchtower in Jerusalem.

In the Old Testament, God presents himself as a husband, and Israel, his bride. She is personified as the "Daughter of Zion." It is a metaphor for a marriage covenant where one person gives himself or herself to the other: "I will make a covenant for them on that day... I will betroth you to me forever: I will betroth you to me with justice and with judgment, with loyalty and with compassion..."[199]

It was unfortunate that the Kings of Israel (after David) married non-Israelite women for they influenced them back into idolatry. We hear God's grief in the words of Ezekiel: "How wild your lust!... Adulterous wife, taking strangers in place of her husband!" [200] In marriage-language, Israel became a prostitute that went with any god who presented himself. It is from this "prostitution" Israel splintered and left Judea as the tribe who remained faithful to the Lord.

Prophets gave Israel a glint of hope when they foretold of someone who would gather the twelve tribes – a way of saying Israel would be brought together again as a kingdom. In Micah, we read, "And you, O tower of the flock, hill of daughter Zion! To you it shall come: the former dominion shall be restored, the reign of daughter Jerusalem."[201]

When we read in Micah that daughter Zion is in labor[202] and from her will come forth the awaited king who will rule Israel,[203] we can understand how it wasn't difficult for the early Christians to

---

[199] Hosea 2:20-21
[200] Ezekiel 16
[201] Micah 4:8
[202] Micah 4:10
[203] Micah 5:1

conclude that Mary is the tangible realization of this allegory. We carry this tradition even today when we say Mary is the personification of *Daughter Zion*.

The "Tower of the Flock" mentioned by Micah, while it is associated with Bethlehem, is also a name for the Holy of Holies in the temple on the hill of the Daughter of Zion in Jerusalem[204] Elsewhere in Scripture, Isaiah uses a vineyard as an allegory for Jerusalem. In the Book of Isaiah, the vineyard belongs to "my beloved,"[205] which can be translated as "David"[206] Thus, the tower – the temple – on the hill is in David's "vineyard," making it David's tower or the *Tower of David*.

So both the tower and the place where the tower is located are a foreshadowing of Mary. We see Mary as this tower for when she was with child, the presence of God was contained in her just as the Holy of Holies did (see *Spiritual Vessel*). From her came the king who would bring together the tribes of Israel in a dominion that would last forever. In this way, Mary is the *Tower of David*.

In another sense, this title also refers to one of the actual towers in the wall around Jerusalem. In olden times, it was important to fortify cities with a wall to keep enemies and marauders out. There were several towers from where sentries could watch for these. When sentinels spotted enemies in the distance, the sentry would warn the head of the guards, and they would close the gates. Soldiers would also rush to the armory so they can get weapons to fight more effectively. The Tower of David was one of these towers. As the main tower, strategists built it to rise above all other structures so it could observe farther than the others.

We get a sense of this tower's fortification from the Song of Songs. It is a poetic rendering of two lovers that are allegories for God as a bridegroom and his beautiful wife. In one of the verses, the bridegroom describes his wife this way: "Like a tower of David, your neck, built with bulwarks; A thousand shields hanging upon it, all

[204] Barker,Margaret. *The Images of Mary in the Litany of Loreto.* P 127
[205] Isaiah 5:1
[206] Wyatt, N. Jedediah *Cognate Forms as a title of Royal Legitimization*, 1985, pp112-125

the armor of warriors."[207] Lyrically, the words express the woman's strength because the trophies of war – the shields of the vanquished soldiers and generals – hang upon her. Because the tower represents a woman, it isn't her brute force that defeats her enemies, but her virtues ("built with bulwarks").

In the Book of Revelation, we read of Christ being a bridegroom to a "New Jerusalem" that is adorned like a bride about to be wed.[208] Throughout the New Testament Jesus often used the wedding metaphor when explaining the "kingdom."[209] This metaphor, of course, refers to the inseparable union of him and his Church: his mystical body – his unblemished bride,[210] which, in the Book of Revelation is symbolized as a "New Jerusalem."[211]

Holding on to that thought for one moment, another metaphor Christ used to describe the church often was a vineyard.[212] In the Book of Mark, Christ told his disciples: "A man planted a vineyard, put a hedge around it, dug a wine press, and built a tower..."[213] It is like the vineyard of David in the Book of Isaiah who also built a tower.

Tying up these two ideas together, if there is a New Jerusalem, and the Church is the New Jerusalem, then Mary is the *Tower of David* of the New Jerusalem. If the Church is a vineyard, then Mary is the tower that the owner built.

King David was a foreshadowing of Christ because he brought the twelve tribes together in a kingdom. Sadly, the realm splintered, but Christ brought it back together in a larger kingdom represented by the twelve apostles. Therefore, if the Tower of David protected King David's kingdom, then it wouldn't be surprising that Christ has his own "tower" in Mary who protects his kingdom.

In a prophetic dream, St. Don Bosco foresaw a ship on a stormy sea as an allegory for the travails of the Church. In the dream, two columns appeared from the waters: one with the Blessed Sacrament

---

[207] Song of Songs 4:4
[208] Revelation 19:7, 22:17
[209] Matthew 9:14-15, Mark 2:19, Luke 5:33-35, John 3:29
[210] Ephesians 5:27
[211] Revelation 21:2
[212] CCC § 755
[213] Matthew 21:33

on top of it; and the other, Mary. In his words, he explained the dream: "Very grave trials await the Church. What we have suffered so far is almost nothing compared to what is going to happen. The enemies of the Church are symbolized by the ships, which strive their utmost to sink the flagship. Only two things can save us in such a grave hour: devotion to Mary and frequent Communion. Let us do our very best to use these two means and have others use them everywhere."

Mary is a tower in this sense when Marian dogmas protect the identity of her son. (See also *Virgin Most Powerful*) When evil is upon us, Mary is our tower because she is endowed with virtues that make her the ever-faithful Daughter of Zion *par excellence* – making her the most effective defense against evil and evil beings whether they are human or spirit. Our Lady revealed to St. Bridget, "On earth there is no sinner, however devoid he may be of the love of God, from whom the Devil is not obliged to flee immediately, if he invokes my holy name with a determination to repent... All the demons venerate and fear my name to such a degree, that on hearing it they immediately loosen the claws with which they hold the soul captive." Our Lady's name is a fortified tower!

As part of the Church Militant, we can fight better when we have spiritual weapons, and Mary is the armory that arms us with graces that she obtains from her Son. As we struggle, Mary should give us peace of mind for we can rely on her because she is the tower that cannot be conquered by the enemy. The enemy tried to poison her, but through God's grace, her Immaculate Conception protected her from the serpent's venom. She has become a frustrating constant reminder to the enemy that his power is limited. So in times of trials and temptation, we should stand behind Mary because God's enemies scamper away in shame as she brandishes her undefiled and inviolate purity as a trophy of their defeat.[214]

When invoking this title, consider that: Mary is the undefeated and invincible protector of Christ's Church.

---

[214] Song of Songs 4:4

TOWER OF IVORY

IVORY HAS THE SAME PROPERTIES AS TEETH. It has an outer layer of tough enamel that has an absolute beauty to its smoothness and flawlessness – which is why it is valued. Inside the hard exterior is pleasant white dentine. Only the wealthy could afford ivory, so it was seen as a symbol of affluence and associated with wealth, beauty, and joyful peace. Its white interior makes it a symbol of purity. With this as context, we can connect it to a verse in the Song of Songs.

The Song of Songs is almost sensually suggestive in how the husband and bride talk about each other, but it is part of the canon of the Bible because it is an allegory for God and his bride, Daughter Zion; and it is also a metaphor for Jesus and his bride, the Church. In the song, the bridegroom passionately declares to his bride, "Your neck is like a tower of ivory..."[215] If we put this on the lips of Christ, he compares the Church's neck to something strong and beautiful.

What is the Church's neck? We start by considering that, as a metaphor, the Church is the Mystical Body of Christ. In Corinth, people were comparing charisms to the point that one claimed his or her charism was better than the others'. Saint Paul had to admonish them through a letter to put a stop to the petty nonsense. He told them that, "As a body is one though it has many parts, and all the parts of the body, though many, are one body, so also Christ."[216] His point is that we are the members of Christ's body and each part has a role to play that contributes to the good of the

---

[215] Song of Songs 7:5 (or 7:4 in other versions)
[216] 1 Corinthians 12:12-16

whole.[217] Thus, we should not envy the spiritual good of others – in fact, it is a sin against the Holy Spirit to do so.[218]

In tying this up with Our Lady, when Jacob had a vision of angels traveling up and down a ladder that reached heaven, the Church sees it as a foreshadowing of Mary. Saint Athanasius, St. Augustine, St. Fulgentius, St. Bernard, and St. Bonaventure see Mary as a spiritual ladder – a means of communication between heaven and earth. Saint Bonaventure intuited that by this *ladder* the Second Person of the Blessed Trinity descended to take our nature. Mary, then, is the ladder by which we receive Christ – the grace of all graces. In the same vein, she is known as the *Aqueduct of Grace*.

Continuing with St. Paul's metaphor, the neck is the part that connects the head and the body. It isn't farfetched to see that Mary as the beautiful neck of the Church when we say she is the *Mediatrix of All Graces*.[219] When God bestows grace, it is dispensed through Mary. Pope Leo XIII explained that every grace that is communicated to this world has a threefold course that is dispensed from God to Christ the head, from Christ to Mary the neck, from Mary to the body that is the rest of the Church.[220] This is why she is also called *Neck of the Mystical Body*. Saint Pope Pius X says it beautifully: "But Mary as St. Bernard fittingly remarks is the 'channel' or, even, the neck, through which the body is joined to the head, and likewise through which the head exerts its power and strength on the body. For she is the neck of our Head, by which all spiritual gifts are communicated to His Mystical Body."[221]

The Catechism says Mary is the preeminent member of the church.[222] That is to say, she is above all other members of the Church. This ties up wonderfully in our metaphor where the highest part of the body, before the head, is the neck.

So Mary is the neck of the Church. However, she isn't just any neck, but a neck "like a tower of ivory" because she is tough, beautiful, flawless on the outside, and pure in the inside. We can

---

[217] Ibid.
[218] The Douay Catechism of 1649, Q915, Q919
[219] Lumen Gentium 62, CCC § 969
[220] Pope Leo XIII. Iucunda semper. 1894
[221] Pope Saint Pius X. Ad Diem Illum. 1904
[222] CCC § 967

hear God speaking to Mary through the words of the bridegroom in the Song of Songs: "You are altogether beautiful, my love; there is no flaw in you."[223]

When invoking this title, consider that: Mary is the beautiful neck of the Church from where God's grace flows to us.

---

[223] Song of Songs: 4:7

HOUSE OF GOLD

FOR MANY GENERATIONS, the Ark of the Covenant traveled with the Israelites to the Promised Land. During their exodus, wherever they stopped to rest, they would pitch a tent for the Ark, and settle around it at some respectable distance.

The Israelites had to combat many enemies, but at one point God gave them rest as they settled down. When peace and flourishing were finally budding in Israel under King David, he realized that he was living in a magnificent palace, while the Ark of the Covenant - were God dwelt - lived inside a tent. So David wanted to build a house for God.[224]

It was almost as if God had a sense of humor when he told David through the prophet Nathan: "Is it you who would build me a house to dwell in? ... I will raise up your offspring after you, sprung from your loins, and I will establish his kingdom. He it is who shall build a house for my name, and I will establish his royal throne forever."[225]

God was talking about Christ who was foreshadowed by Solomon, the son of David who was nursed in swaddling clothes the way Jesus would later be described in the manger.[226] We can say it was witty humor because God did not mean he was going to build a physical house made of granite or marble, but a royal household (like the House of Tudors of English royalty.) God was, of course, referring to the Church, the "house of God" that is made of humans who are the "living stones"[227] that make it up.

---

[224] 2 Samuel 7:2-3
[225] 2 Samuel 7:5-13
[226] Wisdom 7:4
[227] 1 Peter 2:4-5

Nevertheless, David continued with his project, and this house would eventually turn out to be the temple in Jerusalem. David didn't see the house finished, but it was his son, Solomon, who completed it. It was to this temple that people flocked from all over to bring their sacrifices as an offering to God. Temple priests would drain the blood of the animal victims and put their carcasses on a pyre so that the fragrant smell of their roasting fat would rise to heaven.

The Book of Kings details how Solomon overlaid this "house" with gold: "In the innermost part of the house he set up the inner sanctuary to house the ark of the LORD's covenant. In front of the inner sanctuary, (it was twenty cubits long, twenty wide, and twenty high, and he covered it with pure gold), he made an altar of cedar. Solomon covered the interior of the house with pure gold, and he drew golden chains across in front of the inner sanctuary and covered it with gold. He covered the whole house with gold until the whole house was done, and the whole altar that belonged to the inner sanctuary he covered with gold."[228]

This shiny metal is the most fitting material to use because not only is it precious, but it is indestructible. Unlike other metals, no matter how many times gold is melted and reconstituted it doesn't lose anything. Thus, gold can be a metaphor for God in the sense that God cannot be destroyed: in fact, he never changes. Even if God, in the person of Jesus, walks with mankind Christ is still one-hundred percent God. Thus, the term *house of gold* can mean a house that contains gold – a symbolic way of saying a house of God (who is like gold.) Thus, Mary who carried God inside her can be said to be a *House of Gold* in this sense.

However, there is a more significant connection to gold's preciousness in the Litany of Loreto. We aren't told where the gold came from, but it must have been a lot considering how large the temple was. We can only imagine that Solomon must have sourced it from near and far, and he wouldn't go through so much trouble unless he wanted a house worthy and fitting for the Lord.

---

[228] 1 Kings 6:19-22, 7:48-51

On the Immaculate Conception, St. Bonaventure said, "It was becoming that the Blessed Virgin Mary, by whom our shame was to be blotted out, and by whom the devil was to be conquered, should never, even for a moment, have been under his dominion." So when we consider Mary's Immaculate Conception, we can see why she is like Solomon's Temple – a House of Gold – for through the grace of God, she was made worthy and fitting to be the dwelling place of our Lord Jesus Christ.

God's people went to the temple whenever they needed to ask forgiveness or some favor from him. Until today we, the people of God, go to Mary, the new temple, with our supplications so she can intercede for us. Just like smoke arising from the sacrifices in the temple, Mary, our living *House of Gold*, lifts our prayers to God on high.

When invoking this title, consider that: Mary is the living temple who lifts our prayers to God.

ARK OF THE COVENANT

ESSENTIALLY, THE ARK IS A WOODEN BOX CLAD IN GOLD made by following God's precise designs. In it, the Israelites kept three things: the stone tablets of the Ten Commandment, some manna, and the staff of Aaron. Inarguably, it is the most important vessel of Israel because the presence of God manifested itself on top of it. The Israelites felt loved for no other God revealed himself the way theirs did.

The identity of Israel is formed by the idea that they are God's chosen people in a covenant. In the Old Covenant, God gave himself to Israel, and Israel gave itself to God when he said, "You will be my people, and I will be your God"[229] In a covenant ritual, an animal (or several animal victims) are cut in two, essentially separating the lifeblood from the body. Then the parties walk in between the split carcasses[230] as if to put a curse upon themselves that they would end up as the dead animal should they fail to fulfill their part of the covenant.

The Ten Commandments were important to them because they are essentially the word of God written in stone as conditions of the covenant. So, to the Israelites, the stone tablets were symbols of their covenantal relationship with God.

When they were making their way to the Promised Land, the Israelites complained they were hungry, so God made it rain manna. It was some kind of dew that they found on the ground each morning, which they collected and made into bread. It isn't difficult to see why they called it "bread from heaven."

During the Exodus, the appointed High Priest was Aaron, the brother of Moses. The role of the High Priest was to represent the

---

[229] Exodus 6:7, Jeremiah 30:22, Leviticus 26:12
[230] Genesis 15:17

people in prayer and sacrifice. Every year, on the Day of Atonement, the High Priest would go into the Holy of Holies with a bowl of blood from a sacrificed bull. Inside, he would sprinkle the blood on top of the Ark of the Covenant and from above the cherubim figures, in what is called the *mercy seat*, God is said to dispense forgiveness of sins. The High Priest represented the people so when he received forgiveness, it applied to those he represented. Thus, the staff of Aaron represented the priesthood that God gave to humankind – a person who could represent the people in prayer and sacrifice.

The Ark went wherever the Israelites went. When they went to war, they carried it in front of them and won whatever battle they were fighting. Eventually, there came a time when Israel was given rest from its enemies. In this time of peace, King David thought of building a house for the Ark, so it would have a permanent place to stay.

With this in mind, he asked for the Ark to be brought to Jerusalem. The people who brought the Ark made a mistake of using a cart to transport it. God had explicitly instructed that rings be attached to the Ark and poles inserted into them so people could carry it that particular way. At one point in the trip, the Ark began to tip. A man named Uzzah held out his hand to steady the Ark from falling, and he was struck by lightning for this lack of respect for the Ark. Fearing God, David temporarily stopped the delivery and had the Ark stationed in the house of Obed-edom in the hills of Judea "for about three months."[231]

After that time, David asked the Ark to be brought to Jerusalem – this time in the correct way – and sacrificing animals every few steps of the way. When the Ark was finally entering Jerusalem, the people met it with shouts of joy, and David himself danced in front of it as it made its way into the city.[232]

When we read the Infancy Narrative in Luke's Gospel, we can easily see that he intended for early Christians to see Mary as the New Ark of the Covenant. When she visited Elizabeth,[233] Elizabeth

---

[231] 2 Samuel 6:1-11
[232] 2 Samuel: 12-16
[233] Luke 1: 39-56

greeted her with a loud voice just as Jerusalem greeted the Ark with loud shouts of Joy. The unborn John the Baptist "leaped with joy." To *leap* means *to do a whirly dance* and scholars of language like to point out that the Greek word for leap used here is the same verb used when David did his dance in front of the Ark. Finally, "Mary remained with Elizabeth for about three months" in the hill country of Judea just as the Ark did.

The reason why Luke writes this way is that early Christians saw Mary as the personification of the Ark of the Covenant. Just like the Ark that is the source of God's presence among men, so is from Mary that Jesus is *Emmanuel* – God with us.

When she was with child, inside her was Jesus. John refers to him as the *Word* at the start of his Gospel proclaiming, "At the beginning was the Word, and the Word was with God, and the Word was God."[234] Inside Mary were no longer stone tablets on which the "word of God" is written on, but the *Word of God* (with a capital "W") that is a living person who fulfills Jeremiah's prophecy that God would create a people where his laws are written not in stone but "in their hearts."[235]

In the Last Supper, when Jesus told the apostles that the bread is his body, and separately the wine is his blood, they understood its covenantal language when he said, "This cup is the new covenant in my blood."[236] They saw in it the covenant ritual where a victim's blood is separated from its body. However, unlike an ordinary victim in the Old Covenant, this time it is perfected with his own slain body and his own blood. Since he is the High Priest that can be faithful to a covenant that Israel kept failing at, he makes a "new and everlasting covenant" once again fulfilling Jeremiah and Ezekiel's prophecies of a new covenant.[237] If the stone tablets were symbols of the Old Covenant, Jesus is the symbol of the New Covenant. Thus, Mary's womb is the Ark of this "New Covenant."

---

[234] Jon 1:1
[235] Jeremiah 31:33
[236] Matthew 26:28, Mark 14:24, Luke 22:20
[237] Jeremiah 31:31-34; Ezekiel 11:19, 36:26

When the Jews asked a sign from Jesus, he said, "I am the bread that came down from heaven."[238] So also inside Mary was not just manna, but Jesus who is the true bread from heaven. His birth in a manger – a feeding container for animals – should give us a clue that he wanted to feed us his body. The place where he was born, Bethlehem, should also reinforce this when we know it translates to "house of bread."

It is also noteworthy that in Arabic, the translation is "house of meat." Could it be that the Holy Spirit is using language to point us to the Eucharist, which is bread that has become the flesh (meat) of Our Lord?

If so, it shouldn't be difficult to see that the altar of our Holy Mass is not just a place of sacrifice, but a manger where we go to eat Christ in Holy Communion. So inside Mary was not manna that is just some figurative "bread of heaven," but Jesus who is from heaven and came down to feed us with his body in the form of bread. He is the literal bread from heaven!

Just as Adam represented the entire human race in his fall from grace,[239] Jesus is the High Priest who represents the whole human race in his sacrifice to the Father. Through him, we are saved. Thus, inside Mary was not just a rod that represented the High Priest, but the High Priest himself who, in behalf of all mankind, gained the mercy of God's forgiveness.

May I suggest, too, that when Mary was beneath the crucified Christ at Calvary, she was sprinkled with the dripping blood of her son just like the Ark was sprinkled with the blood of a sacrificial victim – but this time Jesus is both High Priest and perfect victim in this definitive and perfected *Day of Atonement*.

Luke was a disciple of St. Peter so his idea of Mary being the Ark of the Covenant was a first-hand inspiration that sprung forth from the teachings of the original apostles. When John wrote the Book of Revelation, he tells of seeing the Ark of the Covenant. This was a high point in the narration because the Ark was missing for many years. Finally, the Ark was found, and he was going to reveal it, but he abruptly stops and ends the chapter. It seems like such an

---

[238] John 6:51
[239] Romans 5:12

anticlimax after the heavens were flashing with lightning and rumbling with thunder[240] as if a drum-roll to unveil the star of the show. However, Bible scholars are fond of pointing out that the books of Scripture were not written with chapter and verse numbers. These were added later on by the scribes. Therefore, if we read the verses of the Ark in the Book of Revelation, the next line is "Behold, a woman clothed with the sun and the moon at her feet."[241] The Ark is revealed no longer as a thing but as a person!

She is in labor and her unborn son is in danger of being harmed by a dragon. It is an apocalyptically styled symbolic representation of King Herod's murderous rage of attempting to kill the child Jesus. It didn't even take one generation after Christ's Resurrection for Christians to see Mary as the Ark of the Covenant – and this from John the apostle himself.

Also remarkable is how in 2 Maccabees, the Ark was taken by the prophet Jeremiah, which he hid in Mt. Nebo where no one could find it. The prophet said that it would be hidden until God gathers his people again and shows his mercy.[242] Applying this to Mary as the New Ark, she appears at a time when God meant to show his ultimate mercy by giving us his only Son who would gather all of us under one Church to whom he would give up his life, suffer, and die for.

The Church gets this typology, and so she sets the feast of the Visitation in the liturgical calendar to coincide with the day Jerusalem would celebrate the feast of the Ark on July 2.

We get our cue on how we should respect Mary from how the Israelites revered the Ark. God gave instructions to the Israelites on how he wanted to be worshipped – a sacrifice of blood upon the Ark. Although God never commanded the Ark to be worshipped, it had to be respected. We see the consequence of Uzzah's actions despite his good intentions.

Christ perfects this blood sacrifice on the cross, which is made present in every sacrifice of the mass. It is how we carry out his

---

[240] Revelation 11:19
[241] Revelation 12:1
[242] 2 Maccabees 2:4-6

command to "do this in memory of me."[243] If the mass is the perfected way we worship God, and Mary is the perfected Ark of the Covenant, we must respect her the way the Ark must be respected. Therefore, Christians throughout the early years of the Church never worshipped Mary, but she was always revered. Catholics continue this today as we honor her with a *hyper-dulia* – a reverence high above all the other saints, but not equal to that of God.

Saint Bernardine said, "When Mary, the Ark of the New Covenant, was raised to the dignity of Queen of Heaven, the power of hell over men was weakened and dissolved." Therefore, as a guarantee of our success against trials, tribulations, and temptations we rally behind Mary as the Israelites rallied behind the Ark in battle. Just as the Ark was directly beneath the presence of God, so was Mary beneath the cross during Christ's crucifixion. It would seem, then, that Mary is inseparable from her son the way the Ark was always near the presence of God. Thus, we can be sure that being near Mary means we are also near Jesus.

We should only be too happy to have her, and so we revel with the psalmist when he exclaims as he makes his way up to Mount Zion: "Arise, LORD, come to your resting place, you and your mighty ark."[244] We likewise rejoice as we make our thorny but passionate ascent to heaven where we shall rejoice in being with our Lord and his might ark, Mary.

When invoking this title, consider that: Mary is the new Ark of the Covenant – the most important vessel of God's people.

---

[243] Luke 22:19
[244] Psalms 132:8

GATE OF HEAVEN

M ARY IS THE GATE OF HEAVEN not because she is our way in; that is Christ's sole role and honor. He is the "narrow gate"[245] if you will – a gate from earth to heaven. Instead, Mary is a heavenly gate, for it is through her womb that the Second Person of the Blessed Trinity passed through to become human. She is a gate from heaven to earth.

From all eternity, God already knew that if he created humanity, we would reject and rebel against him. Archbishop Fulton Sheen had a beautiful way of using a musical analogy for this. He said that if creation was God's opera, man's disobedience was a discordant note. It would be a sour note that would vibrate throughout time and space for all eternity. One cannot undo it. The only way to fix it, Sheen says, is to rewrite the opera so that the sour note is the first note in a new opera.

The "dissonant note" of the fall, is also the first "pleasant note" of salvation. We see this in the Protoevangelium when right after Adam and Eve disobeyed God; he promised the serpent that the woman and her child would crush its head.[246] We see this to be the promise of Jesus, and his mother who, in religious art, are depicted as crushing the serpent's head.

King David, then, is a foreshadowing of Christ. In his battle with Goliath, David was the champion of God's people, while the giant was the champion of the enemy of God's people. After striking down Goliath, David used the giant's sword to decapitate his head.

In the title *Virgin Most Renowned*, we saw how Jael and Judith were instrumental in destroying the enemy by first crushing the head of its leader, and the army finishing off the job. They are a

---

[245] Matthew 7:13
[246] Genesis 3:15

foretelling of the ultimate woman, Mary, who would fight against the enemy of all of God's people – the devil.

From the Protoevangelium in Genesis, we know a woman would be instrumental in God's plan of salvation. God chose Mary and fashioned her through an Immaculate Conception to be fitting for this role. So when God put forth his plan in motion throughout human history, angels must have waited with bated breath for Mary's consent.

When Mary gave her consent, the Holy Spirit overshadowed her, and she conceived Jesus. Thus, the *Feast of the Annunciation* is also known as the *Feast of the Incarnation* that commemorates the precise moment God took on a human form. This is what Catholics believe and is reflected when we celebrate the Annunciation on March 25 – exactly nine months of gestation – before December 25, the day we celebrate Christ's birth.

Every woman who conceives also partakes in a mystery surrounding God for he is the author of life. But this particular conception was different. It was to participate in God's rewriting of a new opera that would correct a bad note. It would not be an ordinary conception, nor would be the circumstances. Through Mary's consent, her womb became the gateway for which God became human.

At the moment of Mary's consent, the crushing of Satan began, for from her the Messiah was born who would ultimately defeat the enemy. Just like David and Judith who used the enemy's own sword to decapitate its head, Christ uses the devil's cruelty and malice to amass blows, strikes, and humiliating insults upon himself (the snake striking at his heel) for the atonement of mankind's sins. (See *Virgin Most Venerable*.) Finally, death – the consequence of sin that was caused by the serpent – took hold of Christ, but whose venom was not strong enough to keep him dead. And so the victorious Christ rendered impotent the deadly poison of Adam and Eve's sin for all of us who follow him. Is that not the fulfillment of God's promise in Genesis?

An unexpected object also foreshadows Mary as a gate. Because Israel was so sinful, Ezekiel prophesied that the *Shekinah* – the glory of God – would leave the temple only to return through the Eastern gate of Jerusalem. It is the gate that faced the Mount of

Olives in the Kidron Valley. Ezekiel saw that the gate would be shut because the Lord entered and it was to remain shut, "and no man shall pass through it: because the Lord the God of Israel has entered in by it."[247]

The Gospels of Matthew, Luke, and Mark all specify the eastern route Jesus took to enter Jerusalem, which could have helped the Jews – who were waiting for the Messiah – to consider him as the promised anointed King. For example, Bible scholars point out that when Jesus was about to enter Jerusalem, the Gospel of Mark puts him east at "Bethpage and Bethany at the Mount of Olives"[248] as an indication Ezekiel's prophecy being fulfilled.

What makes this prophecy a foreshadowing of Mary is that this eastern gate was indeed closed. The Muslims shut it in 810 only to be reopened by Crusaders in 1102. Nevertheless, Saladin permanently walled it up after he captured Jerusalem in 1187.[249] Scholars suggest he knew Jewish tradition, so he had the gate permanently sealed to prevent the Messiah from going through it and thus prevent the city from falling out of his dominion.

If this reason were so, he unsuspectingly fulfilled the prophecy of Ezekiel for Our Lord Jesus Christ, the Messiah, had already passed through it. If Mary's womb is the perfection of that gate, then it was meant to be used only by the Lord and no other human. It is a foreshadowing of her perpetual virginity. This is why Mary is also known as the *Eastern Gate*.

When invoking this title, consider that: Mary's womb is the gate where the Second Person of the Blessed Trinity passed through to become human.

---

[247] Ezekiel 10:18-19, 11:23, 43:1-5, 44:1-3
[248] Mark 11:1
[249] Randal Price, Dr. J. *Rose Guide to the Temple*. Rose Publications Inc. 2013

Morning Star

EARLY CHRISTIANS HAVE USED CELESTIAL OBJECTS as metaphors for some concepts. John uses the sun, moon, and stars to describe Mary as the new Ark of the Covenant in the Book of Revelation for example. (See *Ark of the Covenant*) We celebrate the feast of John the Baptist close to the Summer Solstice when the day begins to get shorter. This is symbolic of John's self-imposed decreasing role when he tells of Jesus: "He must increase, but I must decrease."[250]

Light was always a symbol of God in the Old Testament, as we shall see. When God made his covenant with Abraham, he appeared as a smoking fire pot and flaming torch.[251] In Exodus, it was from a burning bush that God revealed himself when he spoke to Moses.[252] When the Israelites left Egypt, a pillar of fire guided and protected them during the night.[253] In the New Testament, the disciples of Jesus would have understood he was God when he used this symbolism when he said, "I am the light of the world."[254] So Jesus is referred to as the "morning star" because one of the symbols of God is light – and the brightest light in the sky is the sun – the morning star.

Scripture also suggests this very passionately. Scholarly exegesis of Malachi's "sun of justice,"[255] and John's "morning star" in Revelation[256] point to Christ. During Easter the Church praises Jesus when she sings the Easter Exultet: "May this flame be found still burning by the Morning Star: the one Morning Star who never

---

[250] John 3:30
[251] Genesis 15:17
[252] Exodus 3
[253] Exodus 13:21-22
[254] John 8:12
[255] Malachi 3:20 (in non-Catholic Bibles it is Malachi 4:2)
[256] Revelation 2:26-29

sets, Christ your Son, who, coming back from death's domain, has shed his peaceful light on humanity, and lives and reigns forever and ever. Amen."

Because Jesus gave all of himself on the cross, the star is a very appropriate symbol for Christ's self-emptying because a star gives off everything until it collapses and dies. It is the opposite of a black hole, which absorbs everything (like a selfish person would) so that not even light escapes.

Another thing that helped Christians use the sun as a metaphor for Jesus is that it rises in the east. To first-century Jews, the east was a special place for this is where they expected the Messiah to come from. This is drawn from Ezekiel when he prophesied, "and there was the glory of the God of Israel coming from the east!"[257] (See *Gate of Heaven*) Likewise, this is also the reason why altars faced east, and catechumens face east during their baptism.

While Jesus is the sun, for Mary, the title *Morning Star* refers to Venus when it appears in the east just before the sun rises. The order in which the Morning Star appears before the sun is also symbolic because Mary came first before Jesus. Tertullian observed that Adam came first and then Eve followed after she was formed from his side. So in God's poetic redemptive plan to reverse their disobedience and its effects, Tertullian said, it should be only right that the new Adam comes from the new Eve. With this same rationale, he continues, it should be a woman who should usher in the man who would bring salvation.[258]

The coming of Mary prepares to light up the world by declaring that the day of salvation has come. It precedes the coming of Jesus who is to bring the light of redemption upon us.

There is a hymn called the *Akathistos to the Mother of God* that is said or preferably sung while standing. When prayed as part of other works, it can merit plenary indulgence.[259] This would necessarily mean that bishops have approved doctrinal truth

---

[257] Ezekiel 10:18-19, 11:23, 43:1-5, 44:1-3
[258] Tertullian. *On the Flesh of Christ.* 203
[259] Cardinal Ferretto, Joseph. *Manual of Indulgence* # 48, Liberia Editrice Vatican, 1968.

reflected by the prayer. In Oikos 5 it refers to Mary as the *Mother of the Unsetting Star*.[260]

Mary's Morning Star should serve as a reminder that God did not abandon us even after the fall. He planned our salvation, and in that plan, the role of Mary was a crucial part. It was meticulously designed so that Mary had to enter into this world first so that she could bring Christ into it too. This means Mary was not a random product of evolution arbitrarily chosen by God, but specifically selected and fashioned even before the universe was created.

This title gives us a visual image of what kind of light Our Lady is to the darkened human state before Christ. Before the light of Christ brightened this world, her spark – a smaller reflected light – signaled his arrival.

When invoking this title, consider that: Mary is like Venus whose appearance ushers in the sun, the light of the world, Jesus Christ.

---

[260] Akathistos to the Mother of God

HEALTH OF THE SICK

SOLOMON IMPORTED CEDAR WOOD[261] for its strength and fragrance and used them to construct the temple. Since Mary is like the temple that housed the Lord, (see *Spiritual Vessel*) she is associated with cedar.[262]

An older litany invokes Mary as, "Cedar of Lebanon" because there was a belief that the strong odor of cedar can kill serpents.[263] Mary was compared to cedar because, through her consent to be the mother of the Messiah, she became part in slaying the serpent in Genesis – that great adversary of humankind – the devil. The Book of Sirach (also known as Ecclesiasticus) is part of the Wisdom books. As we discussed, early Christians saw Mary as the personification of *Lady Wisdom*. (See Seat of Wisdom) So when the Book of Sirach compares *wisdom* to the mighty cedar and a flowering vine,[264] Saint Bernard easily makes the connection and says, "for as poisonous reptiles fly from flowering vines, so do demons fly from those fortunate souls in whom they perceive the perfume of devotion to Mary."[265]

But cedar has other properties too; it was widely known for its healing attributes. In the Old Testament, for example, God himself told Moses to use cedar as a means of curing leprosy-like infections.[266] It has anti-inflammatory, diaphoretic, expectorant, astringent, anti-microbial, diuretic, anti-asthmatic, and anti-fungal

---

[261] 1 Kings 10:27, 1 Kings 5:10-11

[262] Burkhart, Louise. *Before Guadalupe: The Virgin Mary in Early Colonial Nahuatl Literature*. Institute for Mesoamerican Studies 2001

[263] Ibid. De la Vega, Pedro. 1569:184v

[264] Sirach 24:13, 17

[265] Liguori, St. Alphonsus, *Sermon 60 in Cant.*

[266] Leviticus 14:1-7

benefits. No wonder Egyptians also used in the embalming process of mummies.

Since Mary is the personification of cedar, she is also ascribed with its healing attributes – thus she is the *Health of the Sick*. But there are two sides to seeing sickness: one is physical and the other spiritual. In physical sickness, Mary comes to us as an intercessor for our well-being. The countless miracles in Lourdes attest to this, for example.

In 1858, St. Bernadette was walking by a cave when Our Lady appeared to her. This went on for several days until one day Bernadette asked Mary who she was. Our Lady replied, "I am the Immaculate Conception" – and this at a time and place when and where that Marian dogma was not widely known yet. So it was "proof" that the girl wasn't making things up.

Theologians talk about the attributes brought about Mary's Immaculate Conception. One of the preternatural graces God gave humankind before the fall is freedom from disease and death. This meant that the original design of the human body was not to be harmed by any illness, or to die. However, effects of original sin changed that as it caused the *stain of original sin* inherited by every human. It is not a something, but a lack of something: it is the lack of preternatural graces and sanctifying grace we were gifted with. Thus, the human body gets sick and dies. In short, our nature became sickly.

The dogma of the Immaculate Conception teaches us that God prevented Mary from inheriting this stain. This is why it isn't surprising that another Marian dogma, the Assumption, proclaims she did not die the way we do. Instead, "at the end of her earthly life," she was brought up (the word used is "assumed") into heaven – without suffering death. Therefore, theologians argue if Mary was exempt from death, they suggest that she must also be exempt from disease as they are part of the same preternatural grace. If among all of humanity, she is the only genuinely healthy one among the sick, in that sense she is the *Health of the Sick*.

In Lourdes, Mary also asked Bernadette for a church to be built there and that she "desired many people to come." Since then throngs of people have come and left healed. Thousands of crutches hang on a wall as a testimony to those whose prayers were answered.

The sick sometimes suffer emotionally as well because others loathe them for the difficulty they cause or the unsightliness of the disease. But in Lourdes, Our Lady shows a certain dignity for the sick. It is the same spirit that overshadows Catholic hospitals, usually bearing some title of Our Lady.

We associate her with this kind of care because when Mary allowed herself to be united to Christ's Passion; she knew how it felt like to suffer. Because this makes her compassionate unlike any of us, Mary can fully understand our suffering. She is a creature like one of us, and she feels what we feel. So, in her empathy, Mary's tears fall with ours as she requests her son to stretch out his hand to heal us.

We can be spiritually sick too. In the New Testament, we read about how Jesus healed a leper by touching him. [267] In the Old Testament God told Moses to separate lepers from the general public. Thus, they were isolated and required to ring a bell while shouting, "unclean... unclean."[268] This was imposed to warn people so they could keep their distance as prevention from catching the disease.

While the disease is quite literal, leprosy is also a visual analogy for spiritual sickness. Sin slowly corrupts the soul the way leprosy slowly corrupts the body. Sin disfigures the soul the way leprosy deforms the body. God made us in his image, and so we call him "Abba" – Father (for don't children look like their parents?), but sin disfigures us so much that there might not be enough left for him to recognize us as his children. Sin produces a moral stench the way leprosy causes a rotting odor of the body. Sin is contagious the way leprosy is. Sin merits temporal suffering the way leprosy brings about mental and physical anguish. Sin causes *incurvatus in se* – *a life lived inward*, the way a leper is forced to isolate himself from others. Sin kills the soul the way leprosy eventually kills the body.

Jesus touched the leper even if he didn't need to. He did this to heal the disease and initiate the leper's coming back to society after

---

[267] Mark 1:40-45
[268] Leviticus 13:1-2, 44-46

being untouched for so long. The Sacrament of Reconciliation is much the same way: it is Christ who touches us and cures us in the person of the priest. And so, after confessing to a priest and doing the prescribed penance, we rejoin the Church from which we were separated by sin – very much like how the leper rejoins society in the Gospel.

Continuing with the leprosy analogy, God taught Moses how the cedar can cure leprosy,[269] which is why in the same cedar metaphor, Mary is a cure for our spiritual sickness too.

We go to her when we are too ashamed to face the almighty whom we have hurt. She gives us the strength to go to Christ so he can bring us to the Father who is ready to run and greet us with open arms, a ring for our finger, slippers for our feet, and a roasted fatted calf in the joy of our return.[270]

In both ways, physical and spiritual, Mary is our model of health. She is, as St. Simon Stock called her, *the Medicine of Sinners*.

When invoking this title, consider that: Mary obtains graces for us that keep our fallen human nature resilient from physical and spiritual sickness.

---

[269] Leviticus 14:1–4
[270] Luke 15:11–32

REFUGE OF SINNERS

IN THE OLD TESTAMENT, there was what was known as Levitical cities. God commanded Moses to establish these cities,[271] six of which were "cities of refuge." These were intended as rehabilitation centers for murderers because they could not be punished for their crimes within the city walls. Furthermore, when the high priest died, a special amnesty was granted to these criminals by allowing them to go home untouched.

The *city of refuge* is, of course, a foreshadowing of Christ – our High Priest – whose death heralds our return back to our real home in heaven. Our Lady, who is so configured to Christ, mirrors this characteristic of her son: she is a refuge of sinners in her own way, and likewise prefigured by events in the Old Testament.

When the Israelites journeyed from Egypt to the Promised Land, The Lord preceded them as a column of cloud during the day; and at night, to give them light, by a column of fire.[272] These provided the Israelites a psychological mindset that God was protecting them. Even if their trip was fraught with difficulty, and despite their constant whining, they felt safe behind these columns.

Interestingly, many generations after the Israelites settled in Canaan, the prophet Isaiah foretold of another phenomenon over the temple: "a smoking cloud by day and a light of flaming fire by night. For over all, his glory will be shelter and protection..."[273] He invokes the same imagery of protection the Israelites experienced in the wilderness and used it for the temple.

In the Marian devotion of Orthodox Christianity, Mary is seen as this cloud in the New Testament. She is referred to as the "all-

---

[271] Numbers 35:1-8
[272] Exodus 13:21
[273] Isaiah 4:5-6

bright cloud that unceasingly overshadows the faithful."[274] The imagery of a cloud protecting the faithful people of God in Zion is used for Christians in general. In another symbolic way, it is an image of Christ "coming amid the clouds."[275] Applied to Mary, she is the *cloud*, used as the means of his Incarnation.

As a pillar of fire, St. Bonaventure explained, "...wax melts before the fire, so do the demons lose their power against those souls who often remember the name of Mary, and devoutly invoke it—and still more so, if they also endeavor to imitate her virtues."[276]

For Catholics, our version of the "all-bright cloud" and "pillar of fire" as symbols of protection would be the title *Refuge of Sinners* since we nestle ourselves inside Mary's mantle because it is a place of shelter and safety as we make our journey from this life to the next. This tender and motherly imagery has roots in a Cistercian story.

Sometime in the thirteenth century, a Cistercian monk had a heavenly vision of Mary surrounded by some monks. He felt sad because he didn't see any monks of his order. So he asked Our Lady why his religious order was not there considering their great devotion to her. She answered, "I love my Cistercians so much that I keep them covered with my arms." She opened her mantle, and he saw under it many Cistercian monks.

This story became so popular in Europe that artists drew her cloak wider and wider so that more and more people could fit under it.[277] Eventually, the only way to fit the entire world under her *mantle of protection* was to make the sky her mantle. This is why until today her cape is traditionally blue, and usually decorated with stars.

Churches that are associated with Our Lady have ceilings painted as a sky full of stars. The Notre Dame Basilica in Ottawa, and St. Mary's Basilica in Krakow are good examples of this. Even churches or structures that do not bear Our Lady's name like the Duomo of Siena, the Sainte-Chapelle in Paris, and the Baldacchino

---

[274] *Kanon of the Akathist*, Ode 6, Troparion
  Cunningham, Leslie. *The Cult of the Mother of God in Byzantium.* p103
[275] Mark 13:26, and Revelation 1:7
[276] Liguori, St. Alphonsus, *The Glories of Mary*
[277] Johnson, Kevin Orlin. *Why Do Catholics Do That?*

in St. John Lateran Basilica also have blue ceilings with stars. It should not come as a surprise that before Michelangelo painted the ceiling of the Sistine Chapel, it was blue bedecked with golden stars.

Centuries after the Cistercian story, Our Lady appeared in Mexico where she allowed her image to be forever imprinted on the tilma (the cactus-fiber clothing) of Juan Diego. She is rendered as a lady dressed in a blue mantle ornamented with stars.

Those who've studied the tilma recently found out that the formation of the stars on the tilma was precisely the configuration of the constellations of the sky on the day when the miraculous image appeared – as some sort of proof that the image was not made by human hands.

Through the star-adorned cloak, it is as if Our Lady of Guadalupe is confirming through an image that, "Yes, the sky is my mantle of protection. You can all burrow in it for I am the refuge of sinners." If this isn't enough, she says it in words to Juan Diego, "Am I not here who am your Mother? Are you not under my shadow and protection? Am I not your fountain of life? Are you not in the folds of my mantle? In the crossing of my arms? Is there anything else you need?"

Sometimes we sinners need a place to heal – a place to start anew. Mary is a reflection of God's unconditional love, so she opens her mantle not just to the pious, not only to the saints but also to all of us sinners. There should be no reason, then, why we should have any anxiety about going to her.

Because we can heal under her loving care, she is like a "hospital for sinners"[278] as St. Ephraem rightly calls her. She is also like those ancient Levitical cities where criminals flee for protection. There they could muse on the wrong they have done and how they can begin a new and righteous life. We are reminded that Mary is like that place when we hear St. Alphonsus Liguori quote, "Flee, Adam and Eve, and all you their children, who have outraged God! Flee, and take refuge in the bosom of this good mother. Don't you know that she is our only city of refuge?"[279]

---

[278] Liguori, St. Alphonsus. *The Glories of Mary*
[279] *Ibid.*

When invoking this title, consider that: we can go to Mary when we are troubled about anything.

COMFORTER OF THE AFFLICTED

TOWARDS HIS LAST MOMENTS IN CALVARY, Jesus gave us everything he had: his life, and even after death, blood from his side. But he also gave us the only one thing he could truly call his own: his mother.

Because she understood that she was to be the mother of the Church and that John represented the Church at that moment, they were together until the end of her life. It is, therefore, not surprising that in the Acts of the Apostles we read that she was with St. John and the rest of the apostles during Pentecost.

Catholics consider Pentecost to be the birthday of the Church, because the Holy Spirit, through a strong wind[280] – like a great breath – gave life to the Church the same way the Spirit of God breathed life into the nostrils of Adam.[281] The Church is the household of God[282] and in that house, St. Peter took the fatherly role. We get the word "pope" from "papa," which means "father" because of the fatherly role of the position. But it was Mary who took the motherly role then, and which she now continues to do in heaven.[283] (See *Mother of the Church*)

The fledgling Church was a persecuted church. There were many claimants to the role of Messiah, and Rome put all of them to death – them and their followers. It made sense to eradicate even the followers so there would be no chance of rebellion. This is why the apostles feared for their lives when temple guards arrested Christ.

---

[280] Acts 2:1-4
[281] Genesis 2:7
[282] CCC § 756
[283] CCC § 975

It is interesting to note that scholars believe the Romans did not pursue the apostles because one look at their rag-tag membership would make one conclude they were nobodies who could do any harm. And yet the Church has spread all over the world from this seemingly incapable group – proof that it is the work of the Holy Spirit, and not solely of human effort.

So, as a mother, Mary was there to comfort them in time of great difficulty. The woman who lost her son in the most horrific way was there to provide strength to others despite her own sorrow. It is a demonstration that her means to comfort us does not necessarily always involve removing the affliction, but to make us strong as we experience pain and suffering.

As *Comforter of the Afflicted*, we should look to her as a model who suffered with hope for she did suffer the loss of her son, but through her faith, she was rewarded with the joy of seeing God face-to-face in heaven. We should be consoled that we, too, can meet the same end if we have faith as she does. Shouldn't that give us comfort?

So, as we experience life's turbulent currents, we know we always have a mother to fly to whenever we are afflicted with physical or spiritual pains. As children, we listen to her. As children, we crave to be by her side for she is sure to be near her son. As children, we find strength just knowing our mother is there when we need her.

When invoking this title, consider that: Mary encourages us with hope and strength when we are hurting.

HELP OF CHRISTIANS

FROM DOCUMENTS WRITTEN IN GREEK, we know that the Church
Fathers and early Christians called Mary by two names:
Theotokos (Mother of God), and *Boeteia* (The Helper).[284] John
Chrysostom, for example, used this title in a homily he gave in 345.
Proclus used it in 476, and Sebas of Caesarea in 532.

We can also find written on a third-century papyrus the oldest
documented prayer to Mary. The prayer is the *Sub Tuum
Praesidium* that invokes the help of Mary in battle. The words of
that prayer seem to be the source of the *Memorare* we use today.

The title of *helper* has been used to invoke Mary throughout
the ages but became popular starting in 1571. During the years
leading up to this, Christian Europe was struggling against the
invasion of the Ottoman Empire. The Empire controlled most of
southeastern Europe, western Asia, and Northern Africa – and it
was expanding its borders in the west. Muslim Turks fought their
way to establish strongholds, thus threatening Christianity in
Western Europe.

One such city was Famagusta in Cyprus that the Venetians
controlled. It was a wealthy city and held great commercial
significance. The Empire had unsuccessfully tried to capture it in
prior years. However, with a stronger army and navy, Turks sailed
to the city and bombarded it continuously for almost eleven
months. Christianity suffered a devastating blow when the city fell
in August of 1571.

Not having yet recovered from the defeat, Pope Pius V was
alerted that Turks would launch a naval attack from Lepanto and

---

[284] *World Heritage Encyclopedia* "Mary Help of Christians." Web.
http://www.worldheritage.org/article/WHEBN0017492789/Mary%20Help%20o
f%20Christians , January 2018

sail to Italy. To avert this impending invasion, he assembled Christian armies from all over Europe to defend the remaining Christian nations. Admiral John of Austria would lead the defense and King Philip II of Spain would fund it. While Spain also contributed ships to this effort, the Venetian Republic provided most of the vessels. They were part of the *Holy League* made up of the Republic of Venice; the Spanish Empire; the Papal States; the Republic of Genoa; the Duchies of Savoy, Urbino, and Tuscany; the Knights Hospitaller; and other smaller groups.

The Pope also turned to the Mother of the Church in this endeavor, asking her to defend the Kingdom of her son. So, for this cause, he initiated a prayer to *Mary, Help of Christians.*

Two hundred six galleys and six galleasses (larger galleys) crewed by almost 85,000 men and women sailed from Messina to meet the Turkish threat they knew was leaving from a naval base in Lepanto. On 7 October 1571, the ships of the Holy League met the Ottoman fleet in the Gulf of Patras. The enemy fleet consisted of 222 galleys and 56 smaller vessels operated by a force of 84,000 men and women.

The naval combat raged on throughout the day with the Holy League winning the melees. Though smaller isolated fighting continued until the night, it was clear that the battle went in favor of the Christians. This victory was of great importance because it was so devastating to the Ottoman Empire that it slowed down to a halt any Ottoman military expansion into Western Europe. This naval conflict was to be known as the *Battle of Lepanto*, and the Christian victory there is attributed to *Mary, Help of Christians.*

More than two centuries later, the Church was the target of yet another "invasion." Napoleon I of France took over the powers that be and wanted to use religion as a way to command obedience. At that time, Pope Pius VII had great power too, and he struggled against Napoleon's ideas of using it for his designs of conquest. In 1809, Napoleon invaded Rome and had the Pope kidnapped. He was unceremoniously dragged away over the Alps like a mere commoner. During his journey, the Pope suffered treatment so brutal that his bowels were blocked, he couldn't urinate, and he developed a high fever. A physician who inspected the Pope upon his arrival in Lyon thought it was a miracle he was even alive.

Through the instructions of Napoleon, the Pope was held a prisoner for over five years where he was subjected to trials and humiliation in the hopes the Pope would bend to his will. Napoleon tried to use nefarious methods, for example, by having the Pope injected with morphine. But none of these could break him.

In the Battle of Leipzig, a coalition made up of Russia, Prussia, Austria, and Sweden defeated the army of Napoleon. Subsequently, the Pope was released on 17 March 1814 and was seen as a hero of the Faith for having resisted cruel attempts to make him succumb to a secular power. Attributing the victory of the Church against this "invasion" to Mary's intercession, he visited the sanctuaries of Our Lady where he crowned her images. When Napoleon was finally conquered in Waterloo, the Pope gave thanks to God and Our Lady by declaring May 24, the anniversary of his return to Rome, as the Feast *of Our Lady, Help of Christians.*

In the Old Testament, whenever we read of various nations fighting against Israel, they are allegories of our spiritual battle. The enemy has been and will always be the devil personified as people or nations battling against Israel – the people of God: Goliath, Sisera, and Holofernes, to name a few. This continues in the New Testament with King Herod, and the Red Dragon of Revelation for example. Throughout history, while the face of evil is worn by men and organizations, it is still the devil that is malevolently behind the assaults on God's people the same way he was behind the temptation of Adam and Eve.

Scripture is replete, too, with heroes who arise and stand up to make a decisive blow to the enemy: David, Samson, Jael, and Judith are some of them. They foreshadow Christ, and Mary – the New Adam and the New Eve resolutely fighting the devil. Thus, we can see that Mary is a warrior who goes before us, as the Ark of the Covenant went ahead of the Israelites, to protect the people of God who rally behind her. She had a hand in the Battle of Lepanto, and she had a hand in the downfall of Napoleon. Undoubtedly, she wields her spiritual weapons against those who want to hurt her children, and the Church – the mystical body of her son.

Therefore, when we sense the enemy encroaching on us, whether physically or spiritually, we know we have a champion who fights for us; who sends her mighty angels to protect and defend us.

With Mary as our defender, the devil has already lost, and so he just tries to bring as many with him to his misery. When troubles arise, we need to be happy day after day for we have already won; all we need is to invoke Our Lady's help.

When invoking this title, consider that: Mary continually assists the Church against the attacks of the enemy.

QUEEN OF ANGELS

S AINT THOMAS AQUINAS WROTE EXTENSIVELY ABOUT ANGELS so he is
called *The Angelic Doctor* of the Church. Through his concepts,
we can classify creation into beings that have no spirit such as
rocks and stones; those with matter and spirit such as plants and
animals; those with matter and a spirit that resembles God –
humans; created pure spirits but not divine – the angels. Above all
that, there is also one uncreated pure and divine spirit: God
almighty.

Angels are created spirits that have no bodies to acquire
information, so they were made with full knowledge of the natural
universe. They have free will; thus, nothing gets in the way of their
decision-making. Since they have no bodies, their will is perfect in
the sense that nothing hinders it; unlike humans, whose fallen
nature sometimes makes the body rebel against the will. They are
immortal since they are not made of matter that decays,
deteriorates, or is damaged. We can glean, then, that angels are
powerful spirits capable of doing things that are only limited by
God's permission.

Saint Thomas described their line of command, if you will, as a
hierarchy. There are nine choirs of angels: three groups with three
choirs each. Pope Benedict XVI said that the speech of angels is
actually song,[285] which is why we call their groups *choirs* – a musical
term.

The highest choir is the *Seraphim*, a name that comes from a
word that means *fire* for they are burning with love for God. The job
of the upper choirs is to cascade things down to the lower ones:

---

[285] Ratzinger, Josef. *Jesus of Nazareth: The Infancy Narratives*

Cherubim, Thrones, Dominions, Virtues, Powers, Archangels, Principalities, and Angels.

Saint Thomas liked to say each angel is its own species because each has its own abilities. By usage, we call these spirits "angels," but Saint Thomas reminds us that *angel* means *messenger*. So *spirit* is their nature, and *angel* is their office (work).[286]

Christ is the center of the angelic world.[287] When St. Paul wrote to the Colossians, he told them, "For in him all things were created in heaven and on earth, visible and invisible, whether thrones or dominions or principalities or authorities – all things were created through him and for him."[288]

We read in Scripture about how the angels were present at the birth of Christ singing "Glory to God in the highest."[289] The English translation uses the term "heavenly host," but if we were to translate the Greek word more literally, it would be rendered as "heavenly army." With this closer translation, it is easier to see that they were not there to provide background music, but they were in attendance to serve their king! We also read of times the angels came to minister to Christ: after the temptation in the desert, and during the agony in the garden.[290]

We profess every Sunday that we believe in the "resurrection of the body." This is the belief that at the "End of Time" – a term to denote the return of Christ – our bodies will reconstitute and rise from the grave. Each will then be reattached to its corresponding soul. Because a human did good or bad things with both body and soul, so must a human stand before Christ, the Judge, with both body and soul. Then Christ will give each of us his eternal judgment based on our works.[291] After which, "He will send out his angels with a loud trumpet call, and they will gather his elect from the four winds from one end of heaven to the other."[292] Matthew uses military language to describe how Christ, like a general using

---

[286] CCC § 329
[287] CCC § 331
[288] Colossians 1:16
[289] Luke 2:13-14
[290] Matthew 4:11, Luke 22:43
[291] Matthew 25:31-46
[292] Matthew 24:31

trumpets, calls his subjects to come back to him. Then, "the angels will come out and separate the evil from the righteous."[293] What we want to focus in these scenes is that the angels do what Christ asks them to do.

The angels do Christ's bidding for he is their king. Mary is queen because in the Davidic Kingdom the mother of the king is the *Queen Mother* (See *Mystical Rose*). So if Christ is King of Angels, Mary must be the *Queen of Angels*.

The Ark of the Covenant is a prefiguration of this too. If the Ark, which is designed by God himself, is a foreshadowing of Mary (See *Ark of the Covenant*), then it shows how the Cherubim above the Ark protect her as a means of service to her.

The Catechism does not give details of the fall of the angels except that they did it out of their pride. To make sense of this, theologians suggest that when God revealed to the angels that the Second Person of the Blessed Trinity would be a human, the pride of some angels could not fathom serving a human whose nature is lower than theirs is.[294]

Some theologians even suggest that God may have revealed to the angels that Mary would be queen, which meant they would necessarily have to serve her too. What bitterness might they have because God cannot call any of the angels "mother." What envy might they have because God did not render obedience to any of them the way Jesus did to Mary. What resentment might they have because Saint Michael and his angels can keep fighting Satan, but Mary is the only creature who crushed its head.[295] These theologians suggest that to the prideful angels, serving Mary would be like a human serving a worm that has a nature so much lower than theirs. These supercilious angels found it so repugnant that they chose not to serve. Scholars like to suggest that the number of angels that dissented were "a third" – from the number of stars swept by the dragon in the Book of Revelation.[296]

---

[293] Matthew 13:41,49
[294] Trese, Leo. *The Faith Explained*
[295] Lovasik, Lawrence. *Our Lady in Catholic Life*.
[296] Revelation 12:4

It may seem convoluted that God's revelation of the Son becoming human is what caused the angels to rebel when it is the rebellion of the angels that "caused" Adam and Eve to sin; thus, triggering the plan for God to become human. However, we have to remember God transcends time, so he sees all of history in his present time. To consider cause-and-effect in linear time is a way a creature thinks, unlike the creator who can think outside of that. Besides, we have to remember God did not have to become human to save us: he could have saved us just by willing it. Instead, he chose to become human as a way of redeeming us.

Continuing with these suggestions of theologians, the revelation of God becoming human is a supernatural knowledge in the divine mind that isn't part of the natural universe. Thus, the angels could not have possibly known about it (the same way we would not have thought God is a Trinity unless Jesus revealed it to us.) Angels base their decisions on what they know. Because the knowledge of angels is perfect, there is nothing to change it once they have made a decision. This is why the Catechism tells us that the decision of the fallen angels is irrevocable.[297]

Regardless of what the fallen angels decided, Mary is queen. What was lacking in her human nature is perfected by grace that puts her above all of creation – even above the angels. That is how she is their queen too. No matter how much the fallen angels oppose this; there is nothing they can do against what God has decreed. She is their queen, and because she is queen, the holy angels do what she commands.[298]

Therefore, we can ask our Lady to send her angels to help us, to protect us, and to guide us. It is true we each have a guardian angel,[299] and we can ask for more help from the other angelic spirits who each have their own unique abilities. The enemy tirelessly works in trying to ruin creation, so we must ask Our Lady to aid us with holy angels. They join us, and we join them in this lifelong battle to preserve the earth and save souls.

---

[297] CCC § 392-393
[298] Saint Louis de Montfort. *True Devotion to Mary*, #28
[299] CCC § 336

When invoking this title, consider that: Mary is perfected by grace that places her above the angels who are of service to her.

QUEEN OF PATRIARCHS

THE WORD PATRIARCH comes from a Greek word that translates into today's "head of the family." The Christian family starts with the three great patriarchs: Abraham, Isaac, and Jacob. It is no coincidence that the Gospel of Matthew starts with Jesus's lineage: "Abraham became the father of Isaac, Isaac the father of Jacob..."[300] to emphasize that Abraham is the head – the first member – of the family.

He is considered the first because it was to him God made a covenant with the promise that from him (Abraham) will come forth a great nation.[301] The Lord said, "Look up at the sky and count the stars, if you can. Just so, he added, will your descendants be."[302] Thus, Abram was renamed by God to *Abraham*, which means "father of many." God also promised to Abraham that he would be a great blessing to all families of the earth.[303]

When Abraham's barren wife, Sarai, could not bear him children, she said he could have intercourse with her maid, Hagar. Thinking this was what the Lord had in mind, Abraham did so, and the maid bore Ishmael. However, this was not the son that God promised. As if a rebuke that Abraham used intercourse in his way and not for God's purpose, Abraham and all the males in his family and household must be circumcised. He was also told that he was to conceive a son through Sarai, now renamed "Sarah." It was from her that his descendants would number as the stars.

It was quite a stretch for anyone to believe because he was quite old, and Sarah no longer had her menstrual period. So when a

---

[300] Matthew 1:2
[301] Genesis 12:1-3
[302] Genesis 15:5
[303] Genesis 12:1-3

"stranger" told Abraham that Sarah would get pregnant, she laughed at this impossible birth as if it were a joke.[304] However, the visitor was seemingly stunned at this lack of faith and asked, "Is anything too marvelous for the Lord to do?"[305]

As the Lord promised, Sarah gave birth to Isaac, and it is his lineage we follow, not Ishmael's. Sometime later, God asked Abraham to sacrifice Isaac on Mount Moriah as a burnt offering. So Abraham took Isaac to the base of the mountain and asked him to carry the wood on his back while he himself carried the fire up the slope. Not being told of his role in all this as they made their way up the mountain, Isaac noticed that they had the wood and fire, but there was no lamb to slaughter. He asked his father were the animal for sacrifice was. Abraham's prophetic response was, "God himself will provide the lamb."

At the top of the mountain, Abraham bound his son and took a knife to slaughter him.[306] Scholars like to point out that Isaac must have been a young adult in his late teens or early twenties if he could carry all that wood up the mountain. If that were the case, and if he allowed himself to be bound up, he must have obeyed his father without dissension – like a lamb to a slaughter. We must also point out that it didn't make sense that God would give him a son – the source of the progeny that is as countless as the stars – and then take him away. Regardless, Abraham trusted in God's plan without fully understanding it.

An angel stayed the hand of Abraham and Isaac was spared. Isaac then lived to an age when he could marry. At the age of forty, Isaac took Rebekah for his wife, only to find out she was barren. He prayed for her to conceive, and finally, after twenty years, she gave birth to twin boys: Esau and Jacob.

One day, as a young adult, Esau must have been so hungry that he sold his birthright to Jacob for some lentil soup he made. Having his brother's birthright is one thing, but for Isaac to bestow his blessings on Jacob is another. So one day while Esau was away, Jacob got the blessings from Isaac through some deception. Jacob

---

[304] Genesis 18:1-15
[305] Genesis 18:14
[306] Genesis 22:1-15

was smooth, but Esau was hairy, so Rebekah helped Jacob put on the clothes of Esau and covered him with goatskin. Jacob presented himself to Isaac together with a meal he had prepared. Isaac, already old and blind, mistakenly thought Jacob was Esau when he felt the hairy goatskin and smelled Esau's clothes. Thinking it was Esau in front of him, Isaac bestowed his blessings to Jacob. Later on as if to confirm Jacob's spiritual pedigree, God gave him a vision of a ladder that reached heaven. He told Jacob, "...and in your seed all the tribes of the earth shall be blessed."[307] Thus, we follow the lineage of Jacob, not of Esau.

At the marrying age, Jacob fell in love with Rachel, the younger daughter of Laban. He arranged that in return for her hand in marriage, Jacob would work seven years for Laban. After the seven years was over Jacob married Rachel, but unknown to him she was switched with Leah, Rachel's older sister, as the veiled bride. However, Jacob loved Rachel, so he worked seven more years to wed her.

While Leah gave him sons and a daughter, Rachel had difficulty in conceiving. It took a while before the "barren" Rachel could give birth to Joseph, and to Benjamin as if they were the result of miraculous births. We now focus on Joseph, because he was the product of an almost-impossible birth, and because he was the favorite of Jacob.

The brothers of Joseph envied him and while they were away, decided to kill him. Reuben, one of the brothers, suggested throwing him into a cistern deep inside the earth instead. When a caravan passed by, they sold Joseph to the merchants. Then they smeared goat's blood on Joseph's coat and showed it to Jacob as "proof" of Joseph's "death."

Joseph ended up a slave in Egypt where he interpreted dreams. This was brought to the attention of the Pharaoh because he had a dream no one could understand. Joseph interpreted it as seven years of abundance, and then seven years of famine. He was then given the highest position under Pharaoh, and under that role

---

[307] Genesis 28:14

stored grain during the years of plenty to be used in the years of famine.

When famine struck, Jacob asked his sons to go to Egypt to procure grain as he heard there was plenty there. Unknown to them, it was Joseph who met them. Then, after making sure their "hearts were clean," he revealed himself. His father, Jacob, was so thrilled at hearing that his son, whom he thought was dead, is alive.

We have summarized a good part of Genesis and for a good reason. It is for us to see that from the moment God promised Abraham that he would be a blessing; all generations looked for the fulfillment of this promise. His son, Isaac, and Isaac's son, Jacob, were promised the same as if to reiterate this oath. So, as Matthew listed in his Gospel, father begot a son who begot a son, and so forth, for many generations until he says, "... Jacob the father of Joseph, the husband of Mary. Of her was born Jesus who is called the Messiah."[308]

Mary is the hinge – the turning point – in this lineage of which the blessing of all people finally comes: Jesus, which means "God Saves." Pope Benedict XVI points out that the literal translation of *Yeshua* (Jesus) is *Yahweh saves*. He notes that it is as if God was completing the "name" he gave Moses in the Old Testament.[309] It is a saving name for all people and for all generations. There is no other name by which we can be saved.[310] This is the ultimate blessing.

Mary herself, in amazement and praise to God, proclaims in the Magnificat, "All generations shall call me blessed." She also thanks God because, "He has helped Israel his servant, remembering his mercy, according to his promise to our fathers, to Abraham and to his descendants forever."[311] It is a hymn that closely resembles the one that Hannah sang when she conceived of Samuel. It is a song of thanks to the Lord for remembering his promises for Hannah was barren, and God gave her a child. Therefore, we look at the childbirths too.

---

[308] Matthew 1:12
[309] Ratzinger, Josef. Jesus of Nazareth: The Infancy Narratives.
[310] Acts 4:12
[311] Luke 1:48, 1:55

How could Mary, a virgin, conceive a child with no human father? It is as miraculous as the "impossible" childbirths of the infertile Matriarchs: Sarah, Rebekah, and Rachel. But "Is anything too marvelous for the Lord to do?" the visitor asked Abraham. So we understand it as a lesson that pregnancy is an act of God; and that nothing is impossible for him.

To complete the picture, we must also look at how Jesus figures in all of this. Adam was the original "son" of God for it was God who created him when there was no human father to do so. However, because of the fall, God's plan of salvation was to create a "new generation" – a New Adam, as Saint Paul would call Jesus. It is Jesus who gets the father's birthright just like Isaac and Jacob who also are fruits of miraculous births. At baptism, we are reborn into the Church, and thus, we get this "birthright" too so that we become sons and daughters of God. This is the meaning of our existence – to be partakers of the divine life. It is so central that it is the first thing mentioned in the Catechism.[312]

Mary is seen in the prefiguration of the wives of these three patriarchs. In each marriage, one son represents Christ while the other the human race. Saint Paul, St. Bonaventure, and St. Jerome see one son of Abraham, Ishmael, as a son born of a woman who is a slave, while the other, Isaac, born of a free woman.[313] The bondage of Hagar, the mother of Ishmael, is a metaphor for our spiritual slavery to sin as a result of original sin. Thus, Ishmael is a metaphor for us who are attracted to sin. By contrast, Sarah, the mother of Isaac, was free by nature just as Mary was free – spiritually – by grace, and her son is also free from sin.

Saint Thomas of Villanova saw Rebekah as a prefiguration of Mary especially with the words that describe her: "The young woman was very beautiful, virgin, untouched by man..."[314] which is also how we can describe Mary.

We can also see humanity and Jesus symbolized in her children. For example, Jesus offers himself as a perfect sacrifice that

---

[312] CCC § 1
[313] Thaddeus, Rev.F. *Mary Foreshadowed*, KIC 2015
[314] Genesis 24:16

is acceptable to the Father, the way Jacob prepared a meal acceptable to his father.

It is Saint Augustine who pointed out that humanity is like Esau who sold his birthright for food the way Adam "sold" his birthright for a fruit in Eden. The incarnation of The Second Person of the Blessed Trinity is similar to Jacob who put on clothes and goat's skin to appear like Esau. Saint Antonine reflects that Mary assisted in the Incarnation by making the Second Person of the Blessed Trinity human the way Rebekah assisted making Jacob into "Esau." While Isaac was truly fooled when Jacob took the place of Esau, in the Paschal Mystery, it is as if God allowed himself to be lovingly "blind and fooled" by having Jesus "take the place" of Adam.

Mary is like Rachel too because God loves Mary the way Jacob loved Rachel. She had two sons: Joseph and Benjamin. Jesus is like Joseph in many ways. Joseph was the dearly beloved of his father. Joseph was underground in a cistern, dead to his father, the same way Jesus was dead and buried underground for three days in the tomb. Joseph fed his family grain that is made into bread; the same way God would give the Israelites manna – that bread from heaven – as well as the real bread from heaven, Jesus who feeds us with his body in the form of bread in the Eucharist. When Jacob learned that Joseph was alive, it is as if he was reborn, the way Jesus resurrected as the *first fruit* of the dead.[315]

While Joseph is a prefiguration of Christ, Benjamin is a metaphor for humanity. Jacob named his second son with Rachel, Benjamin, but she called him Ben-oni, which means "son of pain" because of the difficulty in which she gave birth to him that eventually killed her. It refers to the legacy of Eve's disobedience that brought about pain in childbirth that women experience.[316]

Furthermore, when Rachel hid her father's idols, Saint Bernard likes to compare Rachel to Mary who is the destroyer of heresies. The Marian dogmas, for example, secure the identity of Christ from heretical notions. (See *Virgin Most Powerful*)

Saint Matthew draws a similarity between Mary and Rachel too. When Herod sent soldiers to slaughter the innocent children in

---

[315] 1 Corinthian s 15:20
[316] Genesis 3:16

Bethlehem, Matthew says it is a fulfillment of Jeremiah's prophecy of "Rachel weeping for her children."[317] In its original context, the Israelites were taken into captivity and exiled. Knowing the difficulty in childbearing Rachel had, it makes it more poignant that her "children" are taken away in exile. However, the prophecy doesn't end there; Jeremiah continues: "Cease your cries of weeping, hold back your tears! There is compensation for your labor – oracle of the Lord – they shall return from the enemy's land."[318] In the New Covenant context, we see that the death of the innocents has "compensation" for it allowed Jesus to flee to Egypt, the same way Abraham did, and escape Herod's murderous rage. The guiltless children died so that Christ can live and bring all of us into his own "Exodus" to the true Promised Land, which is heaven.

Mary trusted God the way Abraham trusted God. She accepted the invitation to be the mother of the Messiah not entirely knowing all the details. When the time came, her son was put to death the way Isaac willingly went to the slaughter. It is with purpose, then, that Matthew starts his Gospel with the words "the genealogy of Jesus Christ... the son of Abraham,"[319] for Jesus was like Isaac, the son of Abraham, who went willingly to his death. She did not complain, she did not argue; instead, she experienced the Passion side-by-side with her son. This time God did not send an angel to stay the hand of the executioner. This time God provided the lamb, the "son of his birthright," and saw the sacrifice all the way through to the bloodstained end – thus, fulfilling the prophecy of Abraham that God would provide the victim in Jesus. This is why John the Baptist refers to Christ as *the Lamb of God.*

The stories of the patriarchs and their wives all point to the coming of Christ. So how can one say the Bible is a work of human fiction if different inspired writers across 2000 years can write one single story about Christ?

Mary, then, is the archetype of what the patriarchs were prefiguring. Her miraculous birth to Christ is the end to which their foreshadowing serves for she is the queen their stories refer to.

---

[317] Matthew 2:18, Jeremiah 31:15
[318] Jeremiah 31:16
[319] Mathew 1:1

When invoking this title, consider that: the lives of the Patriarchs are in service to tell the story of Mary's birth to the promised blessing, Jesus.

QUEEN OF PROPHETS

IN THE OLD LITANIES, we would ask the intercession of *patriarchs* and *prophets* in one line: "Patriarchs and prophets pray for us."[320] Therefore, it isn't surprising to see Mary's title *Queen of Prophets* follow directly after *Queen of Patriarchs*.

A prophet is a spokesperson of God. The Holy Spirit inspires him or her to tell us what is in God's heart. One of the things the Old Testament prophet also did was speak about future things. It was God's way of giving his people hope. One of these prophecies is that a Messiah will be born of a woman.

When the enemies of King Ahaz of Judah were bent on "tearing Judah apart," they marched upon Jerusalem to do so. When Ahaz and his people heard of this, the entire kingdom was terrified. Through Isaiah, God told Ahaz that the enemy would be themselves defeated. But, "unless your faith is firm, you shall not be firm."[321]

Ahaz didn't seem at all convinced that God would protect them, so Isaiah told him, "Ask for a sign from the Lord, your God." To which Ahaz answered, "I will not ask!" A reply that meant he trusted more on allying himself with the might of the Assyrian Army rather than in the might of God.[322] Isaiah then uttered the prophetic words we read during Advent: "Listen, House of David! Is it not enough that you weary human beings? Must you also weary my God? Therefore, the Lord himself will give you a sign; a virgin shall conceive and bear a son, and his name shall be called Emmanuel."[323]

The name Emmanuel means "God with us," which is a layman's simplistic way of describing the Incarnation. It isn't symbolic

---

[320] *Litany of the Saints*, for example
[321] Isaiah 7:9
[322] Footnotes, Isaiah 7:12, NABRE
[323] Isaiah 7:13-14

language, but literal; it expresses how God wants to walk among his people the way he walked in Eden alongside Adam and Eve. In this context then, the woman that Isaiah mentioned can be no other than Mary.

The prophet Micah also prophesied about the coming Messiah whose verses we also read during the Christmas season. When the Magi were looking for the newborn King, they naturally went to the king's palace. But it was Herod, not Jesus, who lived there.

When the Magi said a star guided them, Herod wanted to look for this king, not to pay homage but to murder him. He asked the chief priests and scribes (to consult scripture) for the whereabouts the baby would be born.

They cite Micah 5:1-3 as the verses that indicate Bethlehem as the place: "But you, Bethlehem-Ephrathah least among the clans of Judah, from you shall come forth for me one who is to be ruler in Israel; Whose origin is from of old, from ancient times. Therefore the Lord will give them up until the time when she who is to give birth has borne, Then the rest of his kindred shall return to the children of Israel. He shall take his place as shepherd by the strength of the Lord…"

Once again, an unnamed woman is foreseen to give birth to someone who will shepherd and bring the scattered tribes of Israel back together. It coincides so well with yet another foretelling by the prophet Jeremiah who said, "Then I will give you shepherds after my own heart, who will lead you with knowledge and understanding."[324] The ultimate shepherd, of course, the Good Shepherd, is Christ; and Mary is the unnamed woman.

This same prophet spoke of the coming home of the tribes. He said that the sign would be that "The Lord has created a new thing upon earth: woman encompasses man."[325] After which he describes a New Covenant: "I will place my law within them, and write it upon their hearts; I will be their God, and they shall be my people."[326]

The modern translation of "woman encompasses man" was translated from the Latin Vulgate of St. Jerome. It is undoubtedly

---

[324] Jeremiah 3:15
[325] Jeremiah 31:22
[326] Jeremiah 31:33

vague, so exegetists look at the original Septuagint text in Greek, which is literally translated as "The Lord has created salvation in a new plantation..." Saint Athanasius uses the words of St. Jerome in the Septuagint phrasing as "God has created a new thing in woman."[327] Understanding the text this way then, Jeremiah tells of a woman from whom a new creation will come forth. This, of course, is our doctrine of regeneration – that Christ saves us as the product of a "new creation."[328] We partake of this in baptism where God brings us to a new life from a state of separation. It is a reference to John's Gospel where he quotes Jesus saying, "... no one can enter the kingdom of God without being born of water and Spirit."[329] When Jeremiah juxtaposes the idea to a new generation with that of a New Covenant, we can be quite sure he is talking about Christ.

The prophets foresee a king. Isaiah addressed Ahaz using the words "House of David" refers to the royal bloodline. Micah says the one to be born will be the ruler of Israel. Jeremiah refers to him as a shepherd, which reminds us of King David who is the original shepherd who brought the tribes of Israel into one kingdom under him. Since the queen in the Davidic Kingdom is the queen mother of the king, the prophets had foreseen their Queen as well. To make things easier, Isaiah said this queen would be part of a "sign" and in biblical terms, "sign" meant "miracle." The miraculous virgin birth undoubtedly points to Mary as this queen.

Because Mary is the queen that prophets foresaw, she is the Queen of Prophets. But since prophets speak the heart of God, saints see Mary as a prophet as well. Saint Irenaeus, for example, wrote that when Mary said her Magnificat, she was a prophet for she "was crying out in the power of the Holy Spirit." One has to read the Magnificat to see how Mary speaks for Israel – revealing that God has kept his promise to Abraham.

We cannot neglect Mary's role as a prophet when she appears from time to time, warning us to repent and do penance. "Penance! Penance! Penance! Pray to God for sinners. Kiss the ground as an act of penance for sinners!" she said in Lourdes. "Pray, pray a great

---

[327] P.G., XXV, col. 205; XXVI, 12 76; The Catholic Encyclopedia, Volume XV
[328] CCC § 1213, 1215, 1262
[329] John3:5

deal and make many sacrifices, for many souls go to hell because they have no one to make sacrifices and to pray for them," she said in Fatima. "The disobedience and disregard of God's commandments are the things that make the hand of my Son heavier...," she said in La Salette.

She is a prophet that continues to speak the heart of God even today in an untiring effort to draw us ever closer to her son, and that, too, makes her *Queen of Prophets*.

When invoking this title, consider that: the prophets foretold Mary would bring forth the promised Messiah.

QUEEN OF APOSTLES

S TRICTLY SPEAKING, Mary is not an apostle, for these were the chosen twelve of Christ. However, the term *apostle* is also used for someone who is called to a particular mission. We read in the Book of Acts that St. Peter and the other disciples evangelized the Jews, while St. Paul's mission was the non-Jews. Thus, he is called the *Apostle to the Gentiles*. He was not part of the inner twelve during the public ministry of Christ but acknowledged as an apostle because of his work. It isn't a small recognition too, for we see him flanked together with the rest of the apostles in the nave of The John Lateran Basilica.

This Basilica is the Mother of all Churches for it is the Cathedral of the Pope. Each Bishop has a Cathedral because there is a chair (which comes from the word *cathedra*) that symbolizes the position of the Bishop who is a descendant of the apostles. Since John Lateran Basilica is the Cathedral of the Pope, it is the chair from which Saint Peter "speaks" and so all other churches around the world are under its care. In short, it is an important cathedral and Basilica.

Inside the John Lateran Basilica are twelve arches: six on each side of the nave. Inside each arch has a statue of an apostle. Judas is not represented, but instead St. Paul is depicted holding a sword for he said, "the Word of God is sharper than a two-edged sword."[330] The arches are made to look as pillars that support the structure of the church – a visual way to show that Christ founded his church on the apostles.[331]

Like St. Paul, other saints are called *apostles* for they had a mission to specific people in parts of the world. Saint Patrick is

---

[330] Heberews 4:12-13
[331] Matthew 16:18

called the *Apostle to Ireland*, for example; and St. Francis Xavier, *Apostle to the Indies*. Because Mary had a mission too, she can be called an *apostle*.

The word apostle means "one who is sent." It is their mission, given by Christ, to "go into the whole world and proclaim the gospel to every creature."[332] Whenever Mary told the apostles anything about Christ, was she not proclaiming the Gospel to them in a way? Wasn't' she giving them more material so they can tell the Gospel better? So in our Catholic small-"T" tradition,[333] we understand Mary as having a mission in the nurturing of the fledgling Church whose mission it is to "go out." (See *Mother of the Church*) We reason that Christ would not have entrusted her as our Mother[334] if this were not so.

The Catholic Church is known to be very meticulous in preserving doctrine, which has not changed at all when compared to what the early Christians believed. We can see what the early Church believed from the writings of the Church Fathers.

We may change the way things are done (our customs), but the doctrine behind them is always the same. This brings us to the point that some people complain a lot about why the Church can't change its views on abortion or contraception but are skeptical as to the integrity of what it believes. Clearly, if it is difficult to introduce doctrinally-foreign ideas into the Church today (like contraception), it would have been difficult to add things contradictory to what it believes from the beginning. If this were true, then it would have been difficult to introduce a devotion to Mary if it had not always existed from the start with the Apostles.

All the apostles took their mission quite seriously as they died as martyrs in their effort to evangelize. Saint John had a different role as he had to take care of Mary.

The Baltimore Catechism referred to the Church on earth as the *Church Militant* for we struggle to evangelize and make our way to heaven. In this line of thinking, the Sacrament of Confirmation

---

[332] Mark 16:15

[333] *Sacred Tradition* is the group of knowledge that, with Sacred Scripture, forms part of the Deposit of Faith – which every Catholic must believe. Small-"t" traditions are those things we hold dear, but not necessarily required of belief.

[334] John 19:27

could be described as giving us weapons for this struggle. In fact, the anointing of the oil on the chest symbolizes giving us a breastplate – just like the "breastplate of righteousness" St. Paul describes in his letter to the Ephesians.[335]

The use of military references reminds us that we are soldiers of Christ whose mission is to expand his kingdom. This was the mission the Apostles understood. In addition, as they went out, it isn't difficult to imagine that Mary was their queen in this endeavor for the kingdom.

When invoking this title, consider that: The apostles looked up to Mary as their Queen in the Kingdom of God.

---

[335] Ephesians 6:14

QUEEN OF MARTYRS

PETER WAS CRUCIFIED UPSIDE-DOWN during the reign of Nero, while his brother, Andrew, was crucified on a cross that resembled an "X." James was beheaded by Herod Agrippa. Philip was scourged, imprisoned, and crucified. Simon the Zealot was also crucified. Bartholomew was skinned alive. Thomas and Matthew were stabbed. Jude and James the Less were beaten to death. Matthias, the apostle who replaced Judas, is said to have been crucified or hacked to death.[336]

We can see why the apostles remind us of martyrs for all of them, except John, died for the Faith. The word martyr comes from the Greek "martur" that means *witness*. They are witnesses because they were willing to give up their lives to defend something they believed in – in this case, the Resurrection of Christ.

Since Mary is the *Queen of Apostles*, and the apostles were martyrs, then she can be called *Queen of Martyrs*. However, she is given this title also because the Saints have seen her as one who "gave up" her life for Christ – thus, a martyr herself.

Saint Bernard said that the Passion of Jesus began with his birth, but with Mary, it started during the Annunciation. When Mary gave her *fiat*, she gave up the simple life she wanted to live. When she brought the child Jesus to the temple, it became clear that difficulties would be part of her life when the prophet Simeon told her "your own soul a sword shall pierce."[337]

Those that study Mary's life count seven swords or sorrows starting with that of Simeon's prophecy. The next sorrow is when she had to escape with Joseph to Egypt, fleeing from the assassins

---

[336] Kelly, Brian. How did the apostles die. Catholicism.org. Web.
http://catholicism.org/how-did-the-apostles-die.html. January 2018
[337] Luke 2:35

of King Herod. The third is when she lost Jesus in the temple – one can only imagine her worry as a mother. The fourth is when she met Jesus as he carried the cross. Fifth is his crucifixion and death. As if his death were not enough, a soldier had to pierce his side – which is the sixth sorrow. Finally, the last sorrow is the burial of Christ – the decisive moment when she had to detach herself physically from the person she dearly loved.

With this, we can understand why scholars can see Mary's life as a prolonged "passion." In art, we often see the Angel Gabriel holding a lily during the Annunciation. The lily is a symbol of purity because Mary was the purest woman ever created by God. For those who see Mary as a martyr, they think of the lily as a sheath with a sword within, for through her *fiat* she exposed her heart so it can be pierced with swords. This is why Mary is also known as *Mother of Sorrows*.

That Mary participated in her son's passion is one of our Catholic traditions. Many saints agree and have said or written beautiful things about it. Saint Pope Pius X said, "It was in the presence and under the very gaze of Mary that the divine sacrifice of our redemption was consummated; she took part in it by giving to the world and nourishing the divine victim..." Saint Alphonsus Liguori wrote extensively on Mary's sorrow and said, "Mary's martyrdom surpassed all others; for it was longer than that of others, and her whole life may be said to have been a prolonged death." Saint Antoninus said, "the sight of her son's torments brought more grief to her heart if she had endured them all in her own person... she consummated her martyrdom by sacrificing the life of her son, a life which she loved far more than her own, and which cause her to endure a torment which exceeded all other torments ever endured by a mortal on earth."

The theologian, Richard of Saint-Laurent, suggested that never was there a mother who more tenderly loves her son than Mary does with Jesus. Even if it sounds like pious talk, it stands up to theological reasoning. True love can come from someone who has no bias, no limits, no constraints, and full knowledge of the person being loved. Since God created Mary without the stain of original sin, she must have infused knowledge that prevented her from any bias – something that was lost for the rest of us as a result of original sin. Her body was in union with her will in full service to God. Moreover, until Christ earned sanctifying grace for mankind so we can be "re-attached" to God, it was only Mary who we can say knew Christ more intimately than anyone for she shared his divine life from the moment of her conception. She had the Holy Spirit dwelling within her that could love as God loves. So when Jesus was tortured, crucified, and buried, there could be no other grief like that of his mother.

Richard of Saint-Laurent very eloquently expressed this when he said, "since there never has been in the world love like Mary's love, how can any sorrow be found like Mary's sorrow?" St. Alphonsus adds that because Mary loves Jesus greater than any other does, "the more bitter and inconsolable was her grief." Therefore, there can be no martyrdom greater than this.

In art, we see martyrs depicted with the instruments of torture used on them. Saint Andrew with a cross, St. Laurence with a gridiron, Saint James the Lesser with a club, Saint Simon the Zealot with a saw, Saint Bartholomew with his flayed skin, Saint Catherine with a spiked wheel, and Saint Sebastian with arrows, to name a few.

The Pieta of Michelangelo is a sculpture of the lifeless Christ on Mary's lap. It is an image of sorrow where we can see Mary as *Queen of Martyrs*. Saint Alphonsus Liguori quoted Diez who said, "Martyrs are represented with the instruments of their suffering... Mary is represented with her dead son in her arms; for Jesus himself, and he alone, was the instrument of her martyrdom, by reason of the love she bore for him."

One must look at the opened hand of Mary in the Pieta for it presents the dead Christ to the viewer. Her hand quietly gestures, "Look, at what my son has done for you." It also proclaims, "This is what I have suffered."

When invoking this title, consider that: the death of Christ made Mary suffer more than the ordeal of any martyr.

QUEEN OF CONFESSORS

WHILE THE WORD "CONFESSOR" CAN MEAN THE PRIEST who hears your confession, it is not what this title refers to; it describes a type of saint. During the time of Christian persecution, many chose death instead of abandoning the faith. It was their way of giving witness to the Gospel. Sometimes, however, some of these holy men and women did not die after being tortured. When they went back to witnessing the faith by their words and actions, they were considered *confessors*.

The use of the term has enlarged over time to be used for one whose sanctity comes from preaching or *confessing* the Faith. It is still the witnessing of Christ, not by giving up one's life as martyrs, but through words and actions.

As Christians, the Faith we profess is that Jesus is the Second Person of the Blessed Trinity who became human, without losing his divinity, died and resurrected so that we might share in the Divine Life. That is the central mystery of Christianity; everything else points to that. Our prayers, our Liturgy, and sacraments mean nothing if Jesus is not God, and if he did not resurrect.

While many men and women are indeed confessors, Mary has been proclaiming Jesus as Lord all her life! In Scripture, there are only three times Jesus speaks to his mother; twice of which she engages him in conversation. In the third, she simply acknowledges quietly.

The first is when she lost and found Jesus in the temple. The method of instruction at that time was for teachers to ask questions, so they saw Jesus in one of these sessions as he was answering teachers. The first thing we need to notice is not that the teachers were astounded, but that both Joseph and Mary were amazed. The Greek word used to describe their amazement is akin to an electric shock. This must have meant that Jesus most probably had not exhibited this sort of brilliance with them at home.[338]

Mary must have known her son was divine because the invitation to be his mother came from heaven.[339] That, and if God asked for her consent, it would not be entirely consensual if he withheld information to the point she didn't fully know what she was consenting to. So if the child Jesus did not exhibit any sort of divinity at home, she must have wondered when he would do so; and could this brilliant display in the temple be the start of it.

As head of the family, Joseph was the one who should have spoken to a son who decided to disappear for three days without telling them. But they knew he was no ordinary child. Maybe that is why it wasn't Joseph but Mary who asked him, "Why have you done this to us? Your father and I have been looking for you with great anxiety."[340] There is no criticism, but merely a statement of their grief.

We should infer from this that Mary treated Jesus differently compared to how mothers managed their children. Yes, she gave birth to him, fed him from her breasts, nursed him, bathed him, and taught him how to speak and walk. He was human after all. However, she knew he was more than just human. She spoke to him in a reverent way that mothers don't usually use with children who go missing for three days. This was her way of *confessing* that Jesus was not just human.

His answer was, "Why were you looking for me? Did you know I must be in my Father's house?" Saint Luke adds, "But they did not understand what he said to them." We have to notice that Mary said "Your father" meaning Joseph; but Jesus said, "my Father" with a capital "F" referring to God the Father. We have to remember that the doctrine of the Blessed Trinity has not yet been fully revealed at this time. In the original Greek, there is no word "house" (some translations use the word "business" also.) Scholars think "I must be at my Father's" is an idiomatic expression indicating the place where the father resides. To us now, it makes sense that the

---

[338] Sheed, Frank J. To Know Christ Jesus.
[339] Ibid
[340] Ibid

Father's house is the temple, but it seemed this wasn't clear to both Joseph and Mary, as they had no concept of the Blessed Trinity yet. Humbly, they accepted they did not understand.

As Catholics, we delight in *mystery* – not fully understanding God. If we fully understood God, then our minds are greater than God. But that can't be, or else we would be God. So we acknowledge that there are things we might understand a bit, but not all of it. Thus, when Luke tells us Joseph and Mary did not understand, it is not because they lacked understanding, but they exhibited a peaceful and humble admittance to the mystery of God. It was a way of confessing Jesus was divine.

The second recorded conversation between Jesus and Mary was at the wedding in Cana. In those days, wine was essential especially for a wedding festivity that can go on for days. So when the wine ran out, Mary perceived the impending embarrassment, so she told Jesus, "They have no wine."

The answer of Jesus in the literal Greek translation is, "what to me with to you woman not yet is come the hour of me." This is such a difficult phrase to understand because there are no punctuations and it can be translated in many ways. One way is "let's leave this alone; my time has not yet come." The problem with this translation is Mary seems to ignore what he said, and tells the servers, "Do whatever he tells you." To ignore her son is not in her nature, so there must be a better explanation. Scripture scholars like the translation, "What is important to you is important to me even if my time has not yet come." It works best with the narration.

It is unlikely for Mary to meddle with Christ's timeline and suggest to him to perform a miracle just out of a whim. No. The Holy Spirit must have prompted her.[341] Through her suggestion, he performed his first miracle that would propel his public life. Through this action, she not only reveals who he is but also gives her son to us.

It is no small action because from that day on he would be a public figure and spend very little time at home with her. This is the great *confession* of her son's identity; while confessors give Christ to

---

[341] Sheed, Frank J. *To Know Christ Jesus.*

those they preach figuratively, Mary gives Christ to the world literally.

The crucifixion of Christ is the last time Jesus is recorded to speak to Mary. Close to his death, he told her, "Woman, this is your son," and to St. John, "son, this is your mother." There is no record of her answering, but we know she acknowledges it because John tells us that from that day on Mary went home with him.

Crucifixion was a cruel death usually reserved for enemies of the Roman state. Jesus was given this penalty because they accused him of disturbing the peace like some insurgent. Anytime there was any treasonous activity, the leader and all the family and members were also put to death.

When Jesus told the apostles they must take up their crosses,[342] they accepted it in its figurative sense. However, when there was a chance of it being literal, they scampered away.

Scripture says darkness came over the whole land.[343] It is during this time of darkness, also in the figurative sense, that Mary remained at the foot of the cross. Her presence there *confessed* her belief in her son all the way, even if it jeopardized her life... even if the situation seemed bleak.

In the Book of Acts, we can see Mary in the midst of the Apostles praying with them as she fulfilled her role as Mother of the Church – the role that Christ gave to her. Her obedience to Jesus by fulfilling this role also confesses his authority.

Today, through her apparitions, she still *confesses* the divinity of Christ. By giving us her son, and by perfectly uniting herself to his wishes, she continually confesses Christ better than any other confessor does.

When invoking this title, consider that: Mary's words and actions communicate her son's divinity.

---

[342] Matthew 16:24
[343] Mark 15:33

QUEEN OF VIRGINS

WE ARE IN THE THIRD TITLE of a group of four titles that declares Mary as Queen of saints. Saints can be categorized into three groups: martyrs who give up their life for the faith, confessors who give their lives to preach the faith, and virgins who give their bodies as consecrated individuals in service of the faith.

While the title *Holy Virgins of Virgins* honors Mary's unrivaled purity, the title *Queen of Virgins* focuses on her elevated position above saints who are classified as virgins. With this, we honor her holy dedication to God.

Even before Christianity, there were virgins dedicated to the service of religion. The vestal virgins of ancient Rome, for example, were priestesses who performed tasks that were off-limits to male priests. It isn't hard to imagine that this influenced christianity since Palestine, where Christianity took off, was under Roman rule.

The notion of virginity as being virtuous came from the persecution of Christians in the first few centuries. Saint Agatha is a good example. A man by the name of Quintianus became enamored with her beauty and forced her to marry him. She turned down every one of his advances because she had dedicated her life to serving the Lord. This, of course, angered him. He was a high-ranking diplomat and had her arrested and brought before the judge. But Agatha had no chance in getting any justice because Quintianus was the judge himself.

In her "trial," he gave her a choice to face torture or possible death unless she married him. When she rejected this proposition, he imprisoned her in a brothel where she suffered for around a month. When that didn't break her, she was stretched on a rack, torn with iron hooks, burned with torches, and whipped. But that didn't lessen her resolve either.

To make her bend to his will, Quintianus ordered his henchmen to cut off her breasts. After the mutilation, she was sent back to prison without any medical attention. The intention was to let her bleed to death.

Saint Peter visited her that night in a mystical encounter, and healed her wounds. When Quintianus found out about the miracle, he still continued to have her tortured. She was stripped naked and rolled over hot coal with sharp shards. The relentless cruelty eventually killed her, but she never gave in to his wishes – wanting to remain a virgin for the Lord.

Another hero of virginity is St. Lucy. Her mother wanted to give her in marriage to a pagan. Just like St. Agatha, she vowed her life in service to Christ. She prayed to St. Agatha, and in a dream, the saint told her that her mother, who was sick, would be cured. Lucy confided this to her mother and persuaded that her dowry should be given to the poor instead – which the mother did.

The rejected bridegroom became vengeful and revealed to the Roman governor that Lucy was a Christian. In this time of persecution, the cruel governor wanted to see if he could break her vow of chastity, so he ordered soldiers to bring her to a brothel. When she told the governor that God would punish him, he retaliated by ordering her eyes to be gouged out.

When the soldiers came to take her, they couldn't move her even if they attached her to a team of oxen. Unable to bring her to the brothel, they gouged her eyes and decided to burn her where she stood. They stacked bundles of wood and twigs around her but found out they couldn't push through with their plans because the wood just wouldn't burn no matter what they did. The only thing they could do was kill her with their swords on the spot, and this they did. When they took her for burial, they discovered that her body was restored as if she wasn't run through at all.

With examples like these, virginity became a noble quality, and the faithful were quick to embrace the virtue. Notable is Saint Thomas Aquinas who told his family he wanted to join the Dominican order. His parents, having a different plan for his life, imprisoned him for over a year. To dissuade him, two of his brothers hired a prostitute to seduce him. The story goes that he took a fire iron from the fireplace and drove her away with it.

Stories on his life tell of two angels keeping guard over him that night.

Early in Christianity, there was a ceremony that consecrated virgins to our Lord. This fell into disuse during the Middle Ages; however, some nuns in monastic orders maintained the rite. At Vatican II, the rite was revised and now can be bestowed on women living in a monastic order, or on women "in the world." This was done to revive the form of life that had been found early in the Church. It is said that it was St. Matthew who initiated this rite of consecration for virgins who lived outside the monastic life.[344]

While virgin saints have raised virginity to a virtue, it was not always that way. In the ancient Jewish thought, having no children was a punishment from God. This is why women in the Old Testament who were barren felt ashamed. This sentiment also crept into the New Testament. For example, when Elizabeth finally conceived, she said, "So has the Lord done for me at a time when has seen fit to take away my disgrace before others."[345] We can feel her shame for not having been able to bear a child before this time.

In the Catholic mind, the turning point of this is the Virgin Mary. Pope Benedict XVI said she is the first sacred virgin who was "consecrated" by the Holy Spirit during the Annunciation.[346] From the *Protoevangelium of James*, we learn that Mary had wanted to live as a virgin dedicated to the temple, the dwelling place of God. However, when she gave her consent to be the mother of the Messiah, she devoted her life not just to the dwelling place of God, but also to God himself. It should boggle the mind that she became the temple itself for God dwelled in her womb for nine months – and all these while remaining a virgin! Thus, we see her virginity as the highest level of humanity and therefore, elevates her above all virgins.

When invoking this title, consider that: those who dedicate their virginity in the service of God, look up to Mary as their model of this commitment.

---

[344] Diocese of La Cross, *Consecrated Virgins*. Web.
http://diolc.org/consecratedlife/consecrated-virgins/. 2018
[345] Luke 1:25
[346] Pope Benedict XVI. *Address in the International Congress of the Ordo Virginum.* May 15, 2008

QUEEN OF ALL SAINTS

THE CHURCH VENERATES CERTAIN PEOPLE BY CANONIZING THEM and honoring them on an annual feast day in the liturgical calendar. They are called *Saints* from the Latin word *Sanctus*, which means *holy.*

People who die in the friendship of God and are in the joy of God's presence in heaven are saints even if the Church doesn't formally declare them as such through canonization. Some refer to them as saints with a small "s," or *hidden saints.* It is to these saints we dedicate "All Saint's Day" to honor them since they do not have a particular calendar date in which to remember them.

The past three titles proclaim Mary as queen of saints who are either martyrs, confessors, or virgins. This title declares her as queen of these, as well as the hidden saints.

When the Church canonizes someone, she determines if the person has achieved a sense of *heroic virtue.* This is a virtue performed with exceptional promptness, ease, and delight. Basically, virtues are already part of that person's default disposition; they are natural to the person.

One gets these sorts of virtues by a configuration to Christ. We are called to become other Christs, and the way to do that is to configure ourselves to him. We keep hearing that God created mankind in his likeness. The Catechism teaches us that we have intelligence like him. God designed us with a mind that was infused with knowledge, a body that did not perish and is united with the will.[347] With the help of these graces, we were made to resemble God.

---

[347] Trese, Leo. *The Faith Explained*

Sadly, original sin disfigured us so much that we no longer looked like children of God. Thankfully, all the sacraments of the Church configure us to Christ. In baptism, we are made to resemble Christ. When personal sin (sin we commit after baptism) disfigures us, the Sacrament of Reconciliation reconfigures us back to Christ. Holy Orders configures a person to be a priest, prophet, and king the way Christ is. When we eat the Body of Christ in Holy Communion, we become what we eat. These are some examples, but it is always through grace that we are made to resemble Christ.

It is in this sense we can see that saints are "other Christs" who cooperated with grace and reflect his light. Continuing this analogy, Mary is said to be the "moon among lesser stars" referring to how she is most configured to Christ in comparison to the other saints.

Mary's light, we are saying, is not out of her own brilliance, but comes from complete cooperation with God's grace. Grace begets grace, and through Mary's perfect virtue of humility, she "became a heavenly ladder, by which God came into this world.[348] It is from her complete cooperation with God's grace we are given the most magnificent grace of all – Jesus Christ. That alone elevates her status far above all the other saints. Thus, she is the *Queen of Saints*.

When invoking this title, consider that: of all the saints, it is Mary who resembles Christ the most.

---

[348] Saint Alphonsus Liguori. *The Glories of Mary*

QUEEN CONCEIVED WITHOUT ORIGINAL SIN

RIGHT AFTER THE FALL OF MANKIND, God promised the serpent: "I will put enmity between you and the woman, and between your offspring and hers; they will strike at your head, while you strike at their heel."[349]

Enmity is defined as an active hostility towards someone or something. It isn't just a feeling of dislike or aversion. The way God describes this hostility is that it will end with the crushing of the serpent's head.

Irenaeus of Lyons, in his work *Against Heresies*, joins the Church Fathers in interpreting the offspring of this prophecy as Christ, and the serpent as the devil. The Book of Revelation narrates this hostility: a woman and her child are doing battle with a dragon.[350] The child is Jesus and is described here as one destined to rule all nations with an iron rod. It is the portrayal of a king. If the child is Jesus, then the mother is Mary.[351]

Remarkably, the word *dragon* comes from the Greek word that means *huge serpent*. Thus, it is the same serpent in Genesis but this time engaged with the woman and her child in a way that God foretold. In most paintings, we can see Mary holding up Jesus, with the dragon below as if ready to strike their heels.

In Genesis, God said that it was he who would cause the enmity. If Mary was to have any real enmity with the devil, then she should be its total opposite. She could not have true enmity if she were at one time under his influence. Thus, as Catholics, we believe

---

[349] Genesis 3:15
[350] Revelations 21:1-9
[351] Because this is symbolic, the image of the mother can also be Israel who "gives birth" to the Messiah.

God created Mary Immaculate – that is, free from sin and the stain of original sin.

Pope Saint John Paul II said it eloquently: "The absolute hostility put between the woman and the devil thus demands in Mary the Immaculate Conception, that is, a total absence of sin, from the very beginning of her life. The Son of Mary won the definitive victory over Satan and enabled his Mother to receive its benefits in advance by preserving her from sin. As a result, the Son granted her the power to resist the devil, thus achieving in the mystery of the Immaculate Conception the most notable effect of his redeeming work." That we are saved is the effect of Christ's actions, yes, but Mary's total resistance to sin as an effect of the Immaculate Conception is the most notable!

When the Angel Gabriel visited Mary, she addressed her as, "Hail, full of grace." This is an odd greeting because after "hail" is usually the position or name being hailed: "Hail, Caesar" for example, or in the darker years much later "Heil, Hitler." So Pope St. John Paul II says that when Gabriel used these words, it is as if "full of grace" is God's name for Mary.[352] The "name" states her attributes; it is a declaration that she is filled with the grace that we would only receive after Christ's redeeming sacrifice.

It is not an assertion that Mary didn't need saving, but instead, this was how God would save her. That is, the merits of Christ's salvific actions were applied to her in advance. This is possible because God is transcendent of time. That means all of time – past, present, and future – is present to him at the same time.[353] So, for God, the moment of Christ's crucifixion and the moment of Mary's conception are eternally present to him. Therefore, he can apply the graces that Christ merited, (in Mary's future) to her in her conception. This makes Christ also Mary's redeemer the way he is our Redeemer but applied differently.

Why would God do that, we might ask. Because it is "fitting," Pope Pius IX stated in *Ineffabilis Deus*. If vessels of the temple were cleansed before they were used, shouldn't the woman who would be the vessel of the Second Person of the Blessed Trinity also be

---

[352] *Redemptoris Mater*, #8,9
[353] CCC § 600

cleansed? Thus, it was "fitting" that Mary's Immaculate Conception made her a suitable dwelling for the Son of God.

We might get tempted to think that Mary's Immaculate Conception was necessary so Christ would not inherit the stain of original sin. No, even without the Immaculate Conception, Christ would not have had any stain of original sin since he is God. Instead, since Jesus is God, he could give his mother any gift he chose; the Immaculate Conception is the gift he gave her. This makes her a human like no other.

When invoking this title, consider that: from the moment of her conception, Mary was made a worthy vessel for the Son of God.

QUEEN ASSUMED INTO HEAVEN

A s CHRISTIANS, Catholics believe that man and woman were
created to live forever with both body and soul. It is a grace that
God gave humanity when he created them.[354] This gift was lost as a
result of original sin. It constitutes part of the stain of original sin
that we all inherit as sons and daughters of Adam and Eve.

Death occurs when the body and soul are temporarily
separated. We say this is temporary because we believe that at the
end of time, when Christ returns as judge, body and soul will be
reunited to stand judgment.[355] From the beginning, our body and
soul were never designed to separate but meant to live together for
all eternity. Sadly, death prevented that as a consequence of
original sin. Since nothing can thwart God's plan, he will bring his
original plan back on track at the *Parousia* – a Greek term referring
to the second coming of Christ. With both body and soul together
forever, those that chose to be with God will be given the joy of
seeing him face to face. God respects the free will of each individual
and doesn't force anyone to be with him if that person doesn't.
Therefore, he will also give those that did not want to be with him
eternal separation from him.

The Church declares some people as Saints. This means their
souls are already in heaven. So, at the resurrection, their remains
will be reunited with their souls in heaven. In short, we are sure
their remains will be in the presence of God. Therefore, as relics, we
honor the remains of saints because we know they will end up in
heaven.

---

[354] CCC § 376
[355] CCC § 366

Relics were important to parish churches too because it would draw people to the church – and that would mean income for the town and for the church as well.

Since Christ ascended into heaven, it means he did not leave any remains. The next best relic, then, would be that of Mary, his mother. So, in the fourth century, the Roman Emperor Marcian of Constantinople, and St. Pulcheria wanted to own the remains of Mary. They searched wide for her remains and even commissioned St. Juvenal, who was the Bishop of Jerusalem at that time, to find it and acquire it for them.

The next conversation they had about this was at the Ecumenical Council of Chalcedon in the year 451 where they all happened to be. There, after his lengthy investigation into the matter, St. Juvenal told Marcian and St. Pulcheria what he found out. He said that:

> Mary died in the presence of the apostles and then they entombed her. Saint Thomas wasn't with them but arrived a few days later. He requested the tomb to be opened to pay his respects – but they found it empty. It is from this that the apostles concluded that Mary was assumed – taken up – into heaven.[356]

This Apostolic Tradition is handed down to us throughout the ages.

Fascinatingly, when Blessed John Henry Newman commented on Mary as the *Mystical Rose*, he likens Mary to the most beautiful flower in the spiritual world. The word *mystical* means *hidden*, so *mystical rose* means *hidden rose*. She is hidden from us, he says, because when her life on earth ended, God took her body and soul where we on earth could not find it.[357] This dovetails well with her title *Ark of the Covenant* because Jeremiah kept the Ark where no one could find it.[358]

---

[356] Saint John Damascene. *Homilies*. Web.
http://www.balamandmonastery.org.lb/index.php/st-john-of-damascus-three-sermons-on-the-dormition-feast. February 2018
[357] Newman, Bl. John Henry. *Meditation and Devotions*
[358] 2 Maccabees 2

Two people in Scriptures were taken up to heaven: Enoch and Elijah.[359] Because the apostles knew this, it wasn't farfetched for them to see how God can take Mary to heaven in a similar way. We know Saint John understood it this way because of how he writes about the "woman" in the Book of Revelation.

In the twelfth chapter, John describes a woman with child doing battle with a red dragon. We can see that the child is Jesus, the mother is Mary, and the dragon is the serpent (see *Queen Conceived Without Original Sin*). He describes how the woman was given eagle wings so she could fly to "a place prepared for her."[360] It is a vision of someone rising above the earth to a prepared place. What is this place that is "prepared" if not an allusion to heaven? We can almost hear the same John when he quotes Christ during the Last Supper: "In my Father's house there are many dwelling places. If there were not, would I have told you that I am going to prepare a place for you? And if I go and prepare a place for you, I will come back again and take you to myself, so that where I am you also may be."[361]

While this forms some of the scriptural basis for the Assumption, theologians also use reasoning to explain it. If Jesus is God, and God is the sheer act of existence,[362] then it would be utterly unthinkable for the Mother of Life itself to be food for worms – the janitors of death. Saint John of Damascus says it eloquently about Mary: "Eve gave ear to the message of the serpent... and together with Adam was condemned to death... But how could death swallow this truly blessed soul who humbly heeded the word of God... How could corruption dare to touch the body that contained life itself? The thought is abhorrent, repugnant, in regard to the body and soul of the Mother of God."

If Mary was immaculately conceived and was sinless the rest of her life, then she is as innocent and justified as Eve was when God created her before the fall. That would mean she did not have to suffer death – or at least a prolonged separation of body and soul.

---

[359] Genesis 5:24, 2 Kings 2:11
[360] Revelation 12:6, 14
[361] John 14:2-3
[362] Aquinas, Thomas. *Summa Theologiae* Ia q44 a.1

Munificentissimus Deus, the document of Pope Pius XII that defines the dogma of the Assumption, states: "She, by an entirely unique privilege, completely overcame sin by her Immaculate Conception, and as a result was not subject to the law of remaining in the corruption of the grave, and she did not have to wait until the end of time for the redemption of her body."

It also states that Mary is joined in a hidden way with Jesus in one and the same decree of predestination, thus, it is fitting that she is preserved free from the corruption of the tomb, as her son is. The Church teaches that at the end of her earthly life, she was assumed body and soul into the heavenly glory.[363]

The Eastern Orthodox Christians, the "other lung" of Christianity as Saint Pope John Paul II calls them, likes to describe Mary's end as a *dormition* – that she "fell asleep." It is a poetic way of illustrating how she closed her eyes and opened them again when God took her to himself.

In most paintings of the Assumption, Christ is depicted as putting a crown on Mary. This is an echo of what happened when Queen Bathsheba entered the court of King Solomon, her son. He stood up, bowed to her, and made her sit on a throne on his right – a position of power. [364] A Davidic king stands and bows to no one but his mother the queen. In so many words, he honored her. Likewise, when Mary entered the heavenly court after her Assumption, Jesus honored her by crowning her – the rightful Queen and *Gebirah* (see *Mystical Rose*) – and made her sit on his right side where she continues to intercede for us to her son. This is why in almost all paintings that have Christ and Mary in it, she is always at his right side (our left.)

When invoking this title, consider that: at the end of Mary's life, Christ took his mother to heaven, body and soul.

---

[363] Pius XII, *Munificentissimus Deus* 44
[364] 1 Kings 2:19

QUEEN OF THE MOST HOLY ROSARY

THE SUFFIX "-ARY" COMES FROM CLASSIC AND MEDIEVAL LATIN that denotes a place of things. *Library*, for example, comes from *Liber*, which means books, and "ary," to designate a place. Thus, *library* is literally, a place of books. Another example is *glossary* that comes from the Latin *glossa*, which is the explanation of a difficult word. *Glossary*, then, is the place in a book where you can find word definitions.

Following this concept, the Latin *rosa* for *rose* plus the suffix "ary" is a place of roses – a rose garden. We find blooming in this *rosary* the white roses of the joyful mysteries, the pink roses of the luminous mysteries, the red roses of the sorrowful mysteries, and the gold roses of the glorious mysteries. These beautiful flowers are important to us because each is a way to reflect on what Christ has done for us. Michelangelo's *Pieta* has the dead body of Christ on the lap of Mary. One of her hands is opened towards the viewer to gesture, "look at what he has done for you." (See *Queen of Martyrs*) The Rosary is the intangible equivalent of that, for we are meant to meditate on what Christ did to save us.

This means the rosary is not just about Mary, but primarily about Christ. We should realize that Christ is in each mystery even if the title does not refer to him. In the Annunciation, we believe Jesus was incarnated in the womb of Mary at the moment of her *fiat*. In the Visitation, the unborn John the Baptism leaps at recognizing his Queen, Mary, and his Lord who is in her womb. During the descent of the Holy Spirit, Jesus was there with his Father as he sent the Holy Spirit down to the Church. In the Assumption and Coronation of Mary, we can imagine it is Christ who takes the hand of his mother up to heaven and there crowns her.

That last mystery hints on what will happen to us who are judged fit to stand in the presence of the Lord. Saint Paul tells us that on our heads will be laid a "crown of righteousness."[365] For us, the crown is but a metaphor, but for Mary, it is real for she is the Queen Mother. Thus, when we say she is *Queen of the Holy Rosary*, it doesn't necessarily mean the rosary is in service to her the way the angels are in the title *Queen of Angels*. Instead, she is *Queen of the Most Holy Rosary* because in it she is the queen that is revealed to us.

Her messages are always those of bringing people closer to her son. In her last apparition in Fatima, the little girl, Lucia, asked Mary who she is and what she wants. Mary's answer was, "I am the Lady of the Rosary, and I have come down to warn the faithful to amend their lives and ask pardon for their sins. Men must not continue to offend the Lord, already so deeply offended. They must say the Rosary."

The title "Lady" is used to address a queen. So when Mary says she is the *Lady of the Rosary*, it is as if she is acknowledging that she is the queen in its mysteries.

It is thought provoking why we call the episodes in the rosary *mysteries*. For Catholics, a mystery is something we seek to understand but acknowledge we cannot fully comprehend. The idea of the Blessed Trinity, for example, is a mystery. Theologians have tried to explain it in a way our finite minds can understand it; most notable is St. Augustine. Despite his great explanations, our feeble minds can never fully wrap itself on how one can be three, and three be one. In the end, we acknowledge some things *amaze* us in the sense that it is above our power of reasoning.

As Catholics, we allow God to astonish us in this way. We even express this concept in the liturgy when the priest uses incense that blurs our vision. Pope Benedict XVI loved to explain that the smoke does not only symbolize our prayers rising up to God but also that our senses are partly obscured to the full greatness of God's mysteries.

---

[365] 2 Timothy 4:8

This brings us to Mary, who all through her life lived and participated in the Paschal Mystery – the entire life of Christ leading to his passion, death, and Resurrection. She must have known more than us for she was infused with natural knowledge. However, she is human and not privy to the supernatural mind of God. Yet, without fully understanding the mystery, she fully cooperated in his plan of salvation – even if it seemed dismal at sometimes (and there were many times – see *Queen of Martyrs*.)

With this full participation, she created room in her life for God to amaze her like no other in history past, present, and future. Thus, if the rosary is the meditation of Christ's salvific actions, then she is the queen in the sense that she participated in its mysteries more perfectly than any person has.

We can join in it too when we pray the rosary. Its repetition is supposed to slow us down and bring us into a meditative state where we can "stop and smell the roses."

When invoking this title, consider that: Mary is the queen in the mysteries of the holy rosary.

QUEEN OF FAMILIES

THE CHURCH IS WHERE WE LEARN ABOUT CHRIST and how to live the Faith. However, children do not encounter the Church right away. Instead, it is within their families they learn about God.

Usually, a child first learns from his or her parents. Like a sponge, the child absorbs words, habits, customs, and traditions. Parents, then, should foster an environment of spirituality where children learn and practice religion. It should be the first school that enriches the idea of what it is to be human both physically and spiritually. This is why the family is vital to the life of a person and why the Church protects it. Since the family is where a child first learns about God, it is what is called the *Ecclesia domestica*, the "domestic church."[366]

If the family is a church, each member is called to be a priest in the sense that each should receive the sacraments, pray, and give witness to Christ in all their actions. Each should offer back to God whatever precious he or she has – that is what a priest does during mass when he offers Christ to the Father. We can see then, that the family should be a "little church."

If the Church is the household of God,[367] the family should be a small version of that. Therefore, if Mary is Mother of the Church, it includes the domestic church. Because Christ is the King of any Christian family, Mary is the Queen mother of the family.

Saint Pope John Paul II put this idea into words on 22 November 1981 in the Apostolic Exhortation *Familiaris Consortio*.[368] There he wrote, "May the Virgin Mary, Mother of the Church, be also mother of the 'family church.' "

---

[366] CCC § 1656, *Lumen Gentium* 11,
[367] CCC § 756
[368] Pope St. John Paul II. *Familiaris Consortio*. Vatican. 1981

Mary is Queen of Families in another sense: she was the mother of the Holy Family. When she accepted to be the mother of the Messiah, it was to be within a family. We know this because Joseph took her, as his wife, into his home.[369]

We know the Holy Family was not well off because when they presented Jesus in the temple, his parents brought two pigeons or turtledoves.[370] Because the Lord saved all the firstborn during the original Passover in Egypt, he said, "Consecrate to me every firstborn."[371] The way to do this was to offer a lamb and a pigeon. But, the law also stated, that if the family couldn't afford it, they could offer two pigeons instead.[372]

God did not provide any miraculous shortcuts for the Holy Family. So theirs was a real family where Joseph did his work and Mary her daily chores. They did not prostrate themselves the whole day on the floor worshipping their son. No. Instead, Joseph was out working, and Mary was doing her part as wife and mother.

Scholars like to note that when the Magi visited, there is no mention of Joseph.[373] The Gospel of Matthew also tells us that they were no longer in a manger or cave but in a house. It also uses the Greek word for "toddler" to describe Jesus. In a Patriarchal culture, it would be insulting not to mention the father of the family if he was there. So scholars suggest that the simple explanation is that the census is over, the Holy Family has moved from the manger to a vacant space in a house in Bethlehem, and Joseph was out working to pay for board and lodging. [374]

From scripture, we know Joseph was a carpenter so we can imagine that he had a workshop. However, in Bethlehem, Joseph was a transient, so he didn't have one. Instead, he went around peddling his services so he could pay for their food and rent. When they went back to Nazareth, we assume he continued his carpentry trade because the people there recognized Jesus as "the carpenter's son."

---

[369] Matthew 1:24
[370] Luke 2:24
[371] Exodus 13:2
[372] Bartunek, Fr. John. *The Better Part.* Catholic Word. 2008
[373] Matthew 2:11
[374] Sheed, Frank J. *To Know Christ Jesus*

Mary, on the other hand, did what most mothers and housewives did. She would have fetched water from the community well early in the morning when it wasn't too hot. Mary would have ground wheat and kneaded flour to make bread in an oven. She would also have sewn and mended clothes for Jesus and Joseph.

Although Jesus is God, we have to remember he is also fully human and had to learn as humans do (but most likely in an elevated capacity.) In the study of Christ, there is a concept called *communicatio idiomatum* (communication of properties). It refers to the two wills of Christ, one divine and one human, which are in constant communication with one another, but with the divine will always operating through the human will.

This means Our Lord had to undergo everything humans had to go through – except sin. There were no shortcuts. Mary had to teach him how to eat, talk, walk, read, and write. When Mary taught him, he wasn't putting on a show just to humor her – he was really learning. It is fascinating that when Mary taught him how to read Scripture, he was learning about himself.[375]

As a human, Jesus learned Jewish tradition and customs from his parents. Jewish boys celebrated their *bar mitzvah* when they reached the age of thirteen. The Hebrew words literally mean "son of the commandment." It is a boy's initiation ceremony into Judaism that marks his readiness to observe religious commandments and participate in public worship. But even before this, we know the child Jesus was absorbing the religious precepts of Judaism from his parents.

When Joseph and Mary found Jesus in the temple, we should not miss that Luke said, "Every year his parents used to go to Jerusalem for the feast of the Passover."[376] By simply going to the Passover, his parents taught Jesus, with and without words, that the Passover was something that every faithful Jew did. Jesus, the all-knowing God, was learning from his parents!

When Jesus was twelve – a year before he was required to go – his parents brought him to Jerusalem during the Passover. It was their way of acclimating him to the religious ceremonies before his

---

[375] Ibid.
[376] Luke 2:41

actual *bar mitzvah*.[377] It was no small matter, as they had to travel by caravan from Nazareth with the larger family – most likely cousins and elders of the clan – for ninety miles over four days.[378] It is fascinating that he would have witnessed the lambs being slaughtered there – something he would himself replace in twenty or so years.

Because the divine nature and human nature of Christ are distinct, we can tell one from the other and define what properties belong to each. However, because there is only one person, the attributes of one nature of Christ can describe the whole of Christ. We can rightly, then, call *Mary the Mother of God* because although Jesus has two natures, one nature is divine so it can be said that the whole of Jesus is divine. Of course, the flipside is true too: because one nature of Jesus is human, we can say that the whole of Jesus is human. This is why we say he is both fully divine and fully human.

With this in mind, we can say that Mary was the only mother whom God obeyed. There is no mother in any family that had that privilege. When Mary told him to do things, he did obey her. How could he, the giver of the commandments, not follow his own commandment to "honor your father and your mother?" After they had found him in the temple, Luke wrote, "he went down with them and came to Nazareth, and was obedient to them…"[379] Such is the humility of Our Lord to place himself under the care and supervision of a human father and mother.

Since Mary is a reflection of her son and his self-emptying, her motherhood was one of service too. In the end, we can see that as the mother of the Holy Family, she was a wife and mother in God's service – even if God was playing on the floor.[380]

This raises her high above all mothers in any family, and that makes her *Queen of Families*. Is there enough evidence in our homes to tell that she is the queen there?

When invoking this title, consider that: we should treat Mary as the queen in our own home.

---

[377] Sheed, Frank J. *Getting to Know Christ Jesus*
[378] *Ibid.*
[379] Luke 2:51
[380] Sheed, Frank J. *Getting to Know Christ Jesus*

QUEEN OF PEACE

O N THEIR WAY TO THE MOUNT OF OLIVES, Peter said, "Even if I should have to die with you, I will not deny you." And the other apostles "spoke similarly."[381] However, they started abandoning Jesus just a few hours later in the Garden of Gethsemane when the soldiers of the High Priest came to arrest him. From the Gospel accounts, we can safely infer that among the select twelve, it was probably only John who witnessed Christ's gruesome Passion and death at the hands of his enemies.

Deep in their hearts, the apostles must have been troubled that they deserted their master at the time he needed them most, especially after they swore they wouldn't. This guilt must have festered in them until it intensified three days later when they heard from Mary Magdalene that she saw Christ who gave instructions for them to meet him in Galilee.[382] Their minds must have been overcome with anxiety at how they would ask forgiveness from our Lord. What kind of face would they have after they had betrayed him? But the next time Jesus was with them, the very first thing he said was, "Peace be with you."[383] He knew their hearts were aching with remorse, so he put them at peace right away. He is, after all, the *Prince of Peace*.

Isaiah foretold of the coming of this prince: "For a child is born to us, a son is given to us; upon his shoulders dominion rests. They name him Wonder-counselor, God-Hero, Father-Forever, Prince of Peace."[384]

---

[381] Mark 14:31-32
[382] Matthew 28:10
[383] John 20:19
[384] Isaiah 9:6

The peace that Christ brings is not just an absence of war, but also a unity. Peace comes from the word *Shalom*, which means, "to be whole." So when King David brought the tribes of Israel together, it was literally "whole" or "at peace."

The peace that Christ brings is also a sense of justice. Justice is the administration of the law, and when King David ruled over Israel, he administered justice dutifully. There was no room for lies, deceit, and corruption. The result of this was a long-lasting flourishing of culture, arts, and a burgeoning economy. Thus, Isaiah was right: peace is brought about by justice.[385]

Peace is one of the fruits of the Holy Spirit. Right after Jesus told the apostles that he would send the Holy Spirit, he said, "Peace I leave with you; my peace I give to you. Not as the world gives do I give it to you."[386] Just as King David brought together the tribes of Israel into one kingdom, Christ brought together the entire world into the folds of the Church – the embryo of his kingdom that is at peace. It is a peace marked with truth, justice, and unity. Thus, wherever we can see these qualities, we can see the work of the Holy Spirit. This is why when Catholics say the Church is "one" it is a claim that the Holy Spirit is its soul that works in her and animates her.

The opposite is true, too. Wherever there are lies, injustice, and a scattering it is from a diabolical source. The root word of "diabolical" is the Greek word *diabelein*, which means to scatter. It is also the root word of "devil" – the enemy whose aim is to tear apart friendships, families, countries, and Christ's one Church.

The reason why we have been talking about Christ so much as the Prince of Peace is that Mary is his mother. Because she is the Mother of the Prince of Peace, in 1917 Pope Benedict XV asked to include the title *Queen of Peace* in the Litany of Loreto.

Interestingly, the First World War was raging at that time, and as if an answer to the invocation, the apparitions in Fatima began. There she asked the faithful to pray, do penance, and the consecration of Russia to her. She was assuming her role as *Queen of Peace* right away.

---

[385] Isaiah 59:8
[386] John 14:27

Right after Christ gave them peace, he said, "Do not let your hearts be troubled or afraid."[387] So in peace, there is a sense of trust that the King is in control. When the king is in control, there is no need for fear. However, if the peace is to continue, there can only be one king in Christ's kingdom. That would mean we would have to relinquish our "kingship" to make way for what Christ wants for us and not what we want for ourselves.

The story of the Magi seeking the newborn Jesus is a lesson for us.[388] The new king threatened King Herod so he wanted to find Jesus to destroy him. In contrast, the "Three Kings" searched for the new king to bow down in deference to him. Different kings; different motives. Our heart is a microcosm of this episode every moment: do we want to destroy Jesus to hold on to our control and remain king or queen, or do we kneel down in submission and trust him to be king?

As we reflect upon Mary in this Litany, her life was not comfortable; in fact, there were a lot of difficulties and sorrows. Despite these and not being able to anticipate the things she was going to face, she nevertheless put her trust in God. By doing this, she was at peace. She is the poster-child of the Psalm that tells us to, "Be still, and know that I am God."[389] This perfect surrender to God must have given her perfect peace, and in this sense, she has achieved it more than any of us have. In this sense, too, we can say she is the *Queen of Peace*.

When invoking this title, consider that: Mary helps us achieve peace by making Christ the king of our lives.

---

[387] *Ibid.*
[388] Matthew 2:1-18
[389] Psalm 46:10

Leave a review
or follow on social media

Thank you for purchasing this book.

Help others know how you liked it. Kindly leave a review at:

http://ourcatholicfaith.net/books/aSkyFullOfStars/review

Let others know about the book. Send them this link:

http://ourcatholicfaith.net/books/aSkyFullOfStars

If you'd like to follow the author to know where he might be touring or get updates on upcoming titles, find his author's page on Facebook:

fb.me/Joby.Provido.Author

If you'd like to follow the author's blog *The Catholic Talks*, you can bookmark the page *www.thecatholictalks.com*

Alternatively, follow the Facebook account:
https://www.facebook.com/thecatholictalks/

Get the Kindle version on Amazon
ASIN B07MJYZD7K

Bibliography

Akathistos to the Mother of God

Aquinas, Thomas. *Summa Theologiae*

Baker, Margaret. *The Images of Mary in the Litany of Loreto.* Usus Antiquior p 110-131. July 2010

Bartunek, Fr. John. *The Better Part.* Catholic Word. 2008

Bouquillon, *Tractatus de virtute religionis*, Brugge, 1880

Burkhart, Louise. *Before Guadalupe: The Virgin Mary in Early Colonial Nahuatl Literature.* Institute for Mesoamerican Studies 2001

Cardinal Ferretto, Joseph. *Manual of Indulgence* # 48, Liberia Editrice Vatican, 1968.

Catechism of the Catholic Church, Liberia Editri Vaticana, 2000 (Abbreviated as CCC)

Ceuppens, C. De Mariologia Biblica, Turin, 1951

Cunningham, Leslie. *The Cult of the Mother of God in Byzantium.* Routledge. 2011

Damascene, Saint John. *Homilies.* Web. http://www.balamandmonastery.org.lb/index.php/st-john-of-damascus-three-sermons-on-the-dormition-feast. February 2018

De Montfort, St. Louis. *True Devotion to Mary.* Catholic Way Publishing, 2013.

Diocese of La Crosse, *Consecrated Virgins.* Web. http://diolc.org/consecratedlife/consecrated-virgins/ January 2018

Erlenbush, Fr.Ryan. *The New Theological Movement*, 12-8-201. http://newtheologicalmovement.blogspot.com/2011/12/was-jesus-immaculately-conceived.html

Encylcopedia of Catholicism 1995

Horvat, Marian Therese PHD. *The Valiant Woman, Petruccia, and the Image of Our Lady of Genazzano.*

Irenaeus, *Against Heresies*

Johnson, Kevin Orlin. *Why Do Catholics Do That?* Ballantine Books. 1994

Kanon of the Akathist

Kelly, Brian. *How did the apostles die?* Catholicism.org. Web. http://catholicism.org/how-did-the-apostles-die.html. January 2018

Labriola, Albert C. and Smeltz John W. *Biblia Pauperum (The Poor Man's Bible)* Facimilie by British Library Blockbook. Duquense University Press. 1990

Labriola, Albert C. and Smeltz John W. *Speculumn Humanae Salvationis (The Mirror of Salvation)* Facimilie by British Library Blockbook. Duquense University Press. 2002

Liguori, Saint Alphonsus. *The Glories of Mary.* Catholic Book Publication Co. Revised Edition.1996

Liguori, St. Alphonsus, *Sermon 60 in Cant.*

Lovasik, Fr. Lawrence. *Our Lady in Catholic Life.* McMillan Company NY. 1957

Newman, Bl. John Henry. *Meditations and Devotions.* Longmans, Green, and Co. 1907

Pope Benedict XVI. *Address in the International Congress of the Ordo Virginum.* May 15, 2008

Pope Benedict XVI. *Jesus of Nazareth: The Infancy Narratives.* Image. 2012

Pope St. John Paul II. *Familiaris Consortio.* Vatican. 1981

Pope Saint John Paul II. *Dives in Misericordia.* 1980

Pope Saint John Paul II *Mary's Relationship with the Trinity.* L'Osservatore Romano, 17 January 1996

Pope Saint John Paul II. *Redemptoris Mater.* Vatican. 1987

Pope Saint John Paul II. *Rosarium Virginis Mariae.* Vatican. 2002

Pope Leo XIII. *Iucunda semper.* Vatican. 1894

Pope Paul VI, *Lumen Gentium.* Vatican, 1964

Pope Paul VI, *Marialis Cultus.* Vatican. 1974

Pope Pius IX. *Ineffabilis Deus.* Vatican. 1854

Pope Saint Pius X. *Ad Diem Illum Laetissimus.* Vatican. 1904

Pope Pius XII. *Address to Women of Italian Catholic Action,* July 13,1958

Pope Pius XII. *Munificentissimus Deus.* Vatican. 1950

Rahner, Hugo. *Mater Ecclesia - Lobpreis der Kirche aus dem ersten Jahrtausend.* Einsiedeln/Köln. 1944

Ralph, Margaret Nutting. *And God Said What?* Paulist Press. 2003

Randal Price, Dr. J. *Rose Guide to the Temple.* Rose Publications Inc. 2013

Sheed, Frank J. *To Know Christ Jesus.* Sheed & Ward. 1962

Sheed, Frank J. *Theology for Beginners.* Angelico Press. 2011

Sri, Edward. *The New Rosary in Scripture.* Servant Books. 2003

St. Prosper of Aquitaine, *Eighth Book on Authority of Bishops*

Strack, H. and Billerbeck, K. *Kom mentarzum Neuen Testamentaus Talmud und Midrush,* vol. 2, C.H. Becksche Verlagsbuchhandlung, Munich 1924

Sulivan, John F. *The Externals of the Catholic Church.* P.J. & Sons. 1918 pp 273-79

Tertullian. *On the Flesh of Christ.* 203

Thaddeus, Rev.F. *Mary Foreshadowed,* KIC 2015

The Catholic Encyclopedia. Nabu Press. 2010

The Douay Catechism, 1649

Thesaurus ecclesiasticus, 1728

Trese, Leo. *The Faith Explained.* Fides Publishers.1965

United States Conference of Catholic Bishops. *General Instruction of the Roman Missal.* Phoneix. 2003

United States Conference of Catholic Bishops. *New American Bible Revised Edition.* Harper Collins Publishers. 2012 (All scriptural quotes come from this unless otherwise stated.)

Wordsworth, William. *The Virgin*

World Heritage Encyclopedia. Web. *http://www.worldheritage.org*

Wyatt, N. Jedediah *Cognate Forms as a title of Royal Legitimization,* 1985

CS-V28

About the Author

JOBY IS A CRADLE CATHOLIC who grew up, and lives in Metro Manila, Philippines where spirituality is high, food is good, and traffic is a bad word.

He teaches web design and development at a local School of Design and Arts where he engages students in conversations about religion, pop-culture, and food.

Each month, he gives short one-hour talks about the Faith under the title *The Catholic Talks* where Catholics and non-Catholics are free to join and ask questions. These sometimes end up longer when students offer him dark chocolate or pizza so he can unwittingly discuss other topics (oh, but he's on to them.)

In an effort to make sure he explains the Faith correctly, he finished his Theology courses on doctrine, scripture, liturgy, and catechism from the satellite program of The University of Notre Dame.

He maintains a website, *thecatholictalks.com*, where he loves to explain doctrine symbolized in Sacred Art.

When he isn't busy with work, he likes to watch movies, sing along to musicals, or attempt to cook Asian food.

41523921R00117

Printed in Poland
by Amazon Fulfillment
Poland Sp. z o.o., Wrocław